PANAMA INVADED

IMPERIAL OCCUPATION VS STRUGGLE FOR SOVEREIGNTY

Compiled and Edited by

PHILIP E. WHEATON

RSP **THE RED SEA PRESS**
Publishers & Distributors of Third World Books
15 Industry Court
Trenton, NJ 08638

The Red Sea Press, Inc.
15 Industry Court
Trenton, New Jersey 08638

Copyright © 1992 Philip E. Wheaton
First Printing 1992

Book design and typesetting by Malcolm Litchfield
This book is composed in New Caledonia and Frutiger

Library of Congress Catalog Card Number: 92-80542

ISBN: 0-932415-67-9   Cloth
        0-932415-68-7   Paper

DEDICATION

This book is dedicated to
the Panamanian people and especially to those killed
and wounded in the invasion. In particular, I want to thank Marco
and Valerie Gandasegui, Xabier Gorostiaga, Mirna Perla de Anaya,
Esmeralda Brown, Kathleen Kennedy, and all my friends, especailly those
working for Panamanian sovereignty
in New York City.

CONTENTS

PART I
Inside Panama: Total War & Its Human Impact

PART II
How Panama's Sovereignty Challenged U.S. Imperialism: Four Crucial Issues that Led to the Invasion

PART III
Panama's Nationalism Under U.S. Colonialism and Regional Implications of the Invasion

INTRODUCTION

Panama
Present and Future

Dr. Marco Gandasegui

When U.S. bombers scarred Panama's cities and 26,000 U.S. soldiers occupied its countryside on December 20, 1989, the nation crumbled. A new colonial government was hand-picked by the United States to steer all public affairs in a way that would satisfy Washington's interests. the old Panamanian Defense Forces (PDF) disappeared and, in its place, a new Public Force was organized by the U.S. Army. A 13,000 man U.S. military machine presently occupies Panama, from its South-eastern border with Colombia to its North-western border with Costa Rica.

The U.S. invasion of Panama cannot be seen, however, solely as a military operation. Prior to this massive attack against the least-populated country of Latin America, the United States had already severely undermined its social structures and penetrated its security defenses. These measures worsened the country's economic and social crisis, which during the 1980s experienced a profound economic recession, similar to that of the 1930s. This recession practically wiped out the country's productive activities, which were adversely affected by U.S. pressures (from the IMF and World Bank), forcing Panama to abandon its development strategies. Unemployment climbed from a figure of 9% in 1979 to 22% in 1988, just before the U.S. sanctions were applied.

The economic sanctions ordered by the Reagan decree delivered a devastating blow to the economy. Unemployment soared to 30% of Panama's working population while another 30% was forced to join the so-called "informal sector" (part-time and street labor). What had been a relatively prosperous economy between 1955 and 1975 (an annual growth rate of 10%) had been destroyed by a slow process of strangulation, described by Senator d'Amato as a "strike at the jugular vein."

The United States was also militant in its efforts to isolate Panama from its Latin American neighbors, its non-aligned friends in the Third World, and from Europe and Japan. The policy was designed to unravel the international consensus that Panama had built up in support of its demands for new Canal treaties, as well as for a new correlation of forces in Central America. Throughout the latter part of the 1980s, Panama's regional policies and projections (including Contadora) were torn apart by the Reagan and Bush administrations.

In this book, you will find a host of interpretations dealing with the invasion, U.S. policy vis-à-vis Panama and the country's military occupation. It is important that the reader place these issues in context. For this reason, I raise three crucial questions. First, what happened in Panama? Where did the Panamanians flounder? Second, why did the United States chose a militaristic solution to its differences with Panama? How long will its Army continue to occupy the Isthmus? Third, what alternatives are open for action to the Panamanian people? Can Panama rebuild its sovereign institutions? Can the people, after such a tragedy, recover and set a course towards a nation free of military intervention and respectful of human dignity?

Why Did Panama Fall So Easily?

A small nation must stand united in order to face internal as well as external challenges. On the basis of national unity, a society of men and women can rally together. For example, in spite of internal strife and class conflicts, during the post-World War II period, the Panamanian people were bent on promoting development that would benefit everyone. This economic development was closely associated with the national recovery of the Canal and the closing down of the U.S. military bases. This "nationalist" feeling was especially strong and expanding between 1947 and 1977.

After the approval of the 1977 Canal treaties and then with the extended economic recession of the 1980s, this nationalism began to weaken. On the other hand, the populace expected immediate results from the new treaties. When these were not forthcoming, frustration set in. On the other hand, economic recession weakened prospects for new and better opportunities across class lines: among business, the middle-class and workers.

Instead of facing the question seriously, the Panamanian government and leadership chose to abandon its previous development policies and set a course masterminded by the World Bank and IMF. This meant shifting emphasis from productive investments to service activities. The economic consequence was increased unemployment. Politically, these same policies drove a wedge between the member groups of the "national" alliance. Furthermore, the role of the PDF was enhanced in order to guarantee social order endangered by the new economic policy. Another important decision was made: with the implementation of the treaty in the year 2000 (which would culminate in a U.S. evacuation), *Canal defense would be turned over to the PDF.*

The PDF believed it could outmaneuver the U.S. government due to its previous close partnership with Washington's intelligence agencies. Based on this assumption, the PDF failed to act in the best interests of the country. Only after Reagan announced economic sanctions in April 1988, did the PDF call for a National Unity Front. The initiative was too little and too late.

By late 1988, the PDF had concentrated all political power in its hands and had converted governmental political parties into mere appendages, utilizing the splintered popular movement as an instrument to gain whatever support it could find at the international level.

The opposition parties and the Crusade were not able to destabilize the government due to one fundamental reason: *they did not want to mobilize the Panamanian people.* As a matter of fact, they were aware that a general mobilization would have brought about the downfall of the top military echelon, but that would also have given the popular organizations a voice in the political process.

After the May 1989 elections were invalidated, the country was in disarray. The government and the PDF had lost all legitimacy. The opposition as well as the Crusade never wanted to mobilize the people and the popular movement was completely helpless. The economy was in "shambles," as Reagan proudly put it, before leaving office. The stage was set, therefore, for the worst, and as expected, the worst occurred.

Why Did the United States Chose a Military Solution?

The United States has many means at its command to accomplish its goals, as the most powerful nation on earth. Washington has had—for well over a century—important political interests and assets in Panama, as well as being deeply involved in its internal affairs. On several occasions, it has sent troops into Panama in order to maintain its domination over the country. However, the invasion on December 20, 1989, represented a display of force in complete disproportion to the goals it had set for itself. The death of between 3,000 and 7,000 innocent people, the destruction of over 6,000 homes and the humiliation of a whole nation, was the price Panama had to pay for its internal division, and, for the hard-headed and narrow-minded attitudes of the military.

Panama's importance to the United States is more than just the Canal which crosses the Isthmus and unites continental America. As the former Louisiana Governor, Huey Long, once put it: "The Panama Canal is the Mississippi's natural mouth to the Pacific." Furthermore, Panama has historically been crucial to U.S. intelligence gathering for all Latin America. And, U.S. Army Intelligence, Navy Intelligence, the CIA, the DEA and the National Security Council have special field teams working 24 hours a day surveying all progressive movements in the continent, in which the Southern Command plays a leading role.

The reason why the United States intervened in Panama was to alter significantly the growing independence between the two countries and to remind both Panamanians and the rest of the world that Washington is in charge of matters concerning hemispheric security. In other words, that no local military organization was going to be allowed to challenge U.S. policy. The PDF's goal of relative autonomy had to be checked. The reasons the U.S. response was so savage is a consequence of the violent contradictions that characterize the relations between the U.S. intelligence agencies.

There has been little fuss and no noise concerning the U.S. military occupation of Panama. U.S. troops are present in every corner of the country. The U.S. Army did the "dirty work" on December 20th and they intend to capitalize on that fact. The U.S. military has set up a political structure aimed at guaranteeing U.S. control of Panama's affairs for a long time. According to the Canal treaties, the U.S. Army would leave Panama by the year 2000, but it is looking towards the future of its presence in the Isthmus. The Army is developing a control by which it alone will decide when to leave or how long to stay.

What Alternatives Are Open to the Panamanian People?

Today, Panama has to deal with two major problems: the U.S. invasion and military occupation and the question of a new national purpose and unity. The more explicit issue is the invasion and occupation, and there is no doubt—at least in historical terms—that the United States will not leave Panama until it is forced to do so. Can a small nation challenge a world power successfully? Apparently so, for it has done so in the past.

The other problem is probably the more important: Can Panama find a road that will lead to national unity and purpose? The experience we have lived through during the 1980s is proof that a divided house will fall when attacked by its enemies. The previous decade of the 1970s, under Torrijos, proved just the opposite. The development policies and strong foreign policy under Omar Torrijos rallied the Panamanian people and brought them together. At the present time, there are no such prospects on the horizon.

So, once again, Panama must find the ideological cement that can muster its people together in search of a common objective that will benefit the whole society. In the past, *this cement has been nationalism* with small ingredients of populism and socialism. Whatever new ideology may be chosen by the people, they must not make the mistake of confusing such ideology with the goal itself, nor the fact that only the people can be the vehicle for such a process.

In such a search, the United States can become a friend or a foe.

Historically, it has always placed itself above Panama's interests, creating havoc and division. The Panamanian people must take this into consideration in order to prepare themselves for a long battle, which includes demilitarizing the Isthmus, creating a strong sense of unity and building a firm economic base, which means capitalizing on its labor force.

We feel the readers of this book will join me in congratulating the editor for his fine work in bringing together so many illuminating contributions to Panama's present reality and future potential.

Panama

October 1991

PANAMA INVADED

IMPERIAL OCCUPATION VS. STRUGGLE FOR SOVEREIGNTY

PROLOGUE

1
Panama's Double Tragedy
Imperial Deceit & Domestic Betrayal

by Philip E. Wheaton, June, 1990

In the aftermath of the U.S. invasion of Panama, a new clarity is emerging among many Panamanians about the motives behind this destructive and immoral action. Many are increasingly clear that Washington's purpose for invading had little to do with General Manuel Noriega, the man—except to use his drug exploits as an excuse. Rather, the main motivation was *to ensure U.S. military control over the Canal and guarantee the presence of its bases in the Zone after the year 2,000.*

As of this writing (Fall 1991), U.S. forces still maintain tight control over the whole country: patrolling Panama's streets and highways, directing its military and police forces, manipulating its colonial puppet leaders, determining its political and economic policies and laying down the propaganda parameters for newspapers and television programs. Therefore, apart from its increasingly sophisticated methods, U.S. goals are the same today as in 1903: *total political and economic control over Panamanian territory considered by Washington to be a U.S. colony.*

Countering this foreign presence and ideology over the years has been the *direct struggle for sovereignty and the indirect resistance to colonialism by the Panamanian people*, a driving force which underlay the events which led to the U.S. decision to invade. It was precisely this struggle that produced the Panama Canal Treaties of 1978, a formal agreement which called for Panama to take over the Canal Zone, a process that was moving inexorably to its conclusion in 1999. The inability of the U.S. government to force the Panamanian Defense Forces to compromise on the bottom-line of those Treaties—Panama's control of the Canal—clearly helped precipitate the invasion.

Yet despite the resoluteness of that earlier struggle for sovereignty (1964-1978), since the death of General Omar Torrijos in 1981, the cause of Panamanian sovereignty has been debilitated and compromised by certain sectors inside Panama who betrayed the struggle. As a result, by last November, many people were saying: "Panama has had it" because of the laws of war set down by the MAN in Washington, but equally because its domestic leadership didn't know how to "convince that river of people—the Panamanians—who have lost their faith."[1] So, we post the thesis that the U.S. invasion of December 20, 1989 represents a *double tragedy*, one that some Panamanians have said has set back the cause of self-determination in Panama by fifty years.

Last November, a newspaper vender on the Via Espana in Panama City reflected on this sad state of affairs by saying: "Tragedy, a national tragedy. They have taken away the 13th from the government. Tragedy."[2] The immediate significance of these words was that Washington's economic sanctions had so debilitated the government that it couldn't pay its traditional Christmas bonus.[3] But in a larger sense, this poor Panamanian worker was reflecting a far greater tragedy that was about to descend upon the country: a military intervention of Panama by U.S. Armed Forces.

We must be clear about this double tragedy, however, in terms of its *primary* versus *secondary* causes, because the basic responsibility for the invasion has been systematically inverted by White House propaganda and placed upon Manuel Noriega. By demonizing Noriega, the Bush administration has justified its invasion to the American public, painting its aggressor troops as "liberators." To be sure, Noriega profited off drugs, was complicit with U.S. agencies and

and abused his power inside Panama, but he was not the demon he has been labelled nor is he the reason for the invasion. Indeed, if we compare Noriega with tyrants like Trujillo in the Dominican Republic or Somoza in Nicaragua, or even with living "pathological killers" like Pinochet in Chile or D'Aubuisson in El Salvador—all of whom were supported by U.S. policy makers over many years without reservation—there is little similarity in terms of sheer evil. Therefore, the real guilt for the invasion lies with those imperial decision-makers who sit in high places in the White House, State Department, National Security Council, Pentagon and the CIA.

The *primary* tragedy of this invasion is that it implies an ongoing foreign occupation which will probably last for years to come. True, this colonial occupation began in 1903 and in one sense has never ended ... a by-product of the transisthmian nature of Panama, or as Gregorio Selser has succinctly described it in the title of his new book: *Panama: You Were A Country Stuck To A Canal.*[4] Panama's history has always been conditioned by its geographical character—as a narrow isthmus between two mighty oceans—which various imperial powers have exploited over the centuries, today the United States.

Ironically, the very excesses of this colonizing process also created Panamanian consciousness of nationhood and from that a growing demand for full sovereignty. North American deceit, racism and economic coercion gradually produced a national repugnance and pride out of which the Panamanian dream for sovereignty developed and came to fruition. It was this indigenous resistance that originally caused the United States to compromise and then negotiate. But after the death of Torrijos, the impetus behind this struggle was reversed and Washington found a number of influential traitors inside Panama willing to collaborate with U.S. interests. Still, many ordinary citizens resisted and held fast to their principles.

It is our conviction that the U.S. invasion of Panama began in 1986, when Adm. John Poindexter issued an ultimatum to General Noriega to resign because he wouldn't fully collaborate with the U.S. strategy to overthrow the Sandinistas and tried to force him to place in the presidency someone pleasing to Washington. This is what the White House calls "democracy." When Noriega refused, the wheels within the National Security Council and State Department began to grind against him, creating economic havoc for the Panamanian people. Therefore, undergirding the invasion dynamic lies an *imperial arrogance*—described so eloquently by what Senator Fulbright wrote about the Vietnam war—which assumes the United States can both use and dispose of foreign leaders at will regardless of the rights or interests of the victim nation.

The *secondary* tragedy about this invasion involves the domestic betrayal of Panama's struggle for sovereignty by certain military and civilian leaders. This process began with General Paredes in 1982, continued with President Barletta in 1984 and certainly included Manuel Noriega as one of those compromising and collaborating with the United States. But the real betrayal began in 1986, and involved members of the Panamanian oligarchy who sold out to the Reagan administration creating the Civic Crusade, and who were known as the *civilistas*. These members of Panama's oligarchy were the ones who fully collaborated with Washington and called for a U.S. intervention. They are the true Benedict Arnolds or traitors of the Panamanian people and nation.

Missing from almost all U.S. newspaper stories or TV interviews is the role of Panama's legitimate democratic sectors who opposed any intervention and defended the right of the Panamanian people to decide its own future. This sector included the legitimate governments of presidents Solis Palma and Francisco Rodriguez (1988-89), as well as those trade unions, student groups and campesino organizations who steadfastly opposed any form of U.S. intervention. True, some of these democratic and progressive sectors went along with pressures from the Noriega military bloc for opportunistic reasons, receiving certain benefits thereby. While Noriega used his power and wealth to buy favors, he was unable to offer any social or political alternatives to the popular masses because of his isolation by the oligarchy and the pressures from the U.S. sanctions.

At the same time, corruption by certain Panamanian military leaders and opportunism by certain democratic and progressive leaders discouraged and disheartened many Panamanians, turning many cynical and leading them to consider the civilista option, but not out of any ideological loyalty nor mass enthuisiasm for that artificially created movement. So this ambivalence in many Panamanians towards the government and Noriega really arose out of popular despair over the extremely harsh economic conditions imposed by the U.S.

sanctions in 1988. It was this combination of hardship and cynicism that led many to accept the consequences of an intervention, hoping it would resolve their crisis.

This secondary tragedy represents a betrayal then, because it made Panama extremely difficult to govern and impossible to defend. As one Panamanian has reflected:

> The laws which direct that social phenomenon we call war shows us that the one who wins is the one who wins over the civilian population; which in good Spanish means that war is fundamentally a political not an administrative nor repressive matter. Thus we must not confuse the "rules of war" with the "causes of war," for when we do we lose the war.[5]

In other words, Noriega lost the war militarily long before the United States invaded Panama, just as the Endara regime has probably already lost the political war of the future by selling out to the gringos. Disloyalty to the people is, then, Panama's first but not its primary tragedy. The real tragedy of the invasion is continued colonial domination and the undercutting of sovereignty promised by the Treaties. Immediately following the invasion on December 20, it was clear that many Panamanians were relieved or elated that General Manuel Antonio Noriega and the Panamanian Defense Forces (FDP) were gone. Also a percentage of them approved the fact the U. S. military had intervened. During that period, a T-shirt was widely distributed in Panama which carried the gringo slogan "Just Cause" attempting to justify Washington's foreign occupation. Since then, however, popular sentiment has labelled the invasion "Operation Injustice," while enthusiasm for the presence of U.S. troops patrolling the streets of Panama has disappeared.

In spite of the overwhelming numbers and fire-power of the U.S. forces, Panamanians resisted the gringos during the invasion more than Pentagon officials had anticipated, evidenced by the deaths of 23 North American soldiers. More recently, other expressions of resistance to the U.S. occupation have emerged: workers' protests, public marches demanding indemnization for destroyed homes and violent attacks on U.S. soldiers. So things are clearer now in Panama. The democratic and popular forces are clearer; students and workers are much clearer now. This resistance is resurrecting the symbolic heros of yesterday, such as the students who challenged U.S. colonialism back in 1964.[6]

In the sobering aftermath of the invasion, many Panamanians are reflecting on how to restore their independence in the face of this new expression of imperial domination. As the legendary General Omar Torrijos said, following the frustrated attempt by members of the oligarchy together with certain U.S. embassy personnel to overthrow his revolution in 1969:

> Now, no one can hold back the democratic principles of the October takeover (1968), because the reactionary pressures against our revolutionary government cannot hold back this march without limits—our convictions and republican principles—which have as their only objective the well-being of all Panamanians without distinction as to political creed or allegiance.[7]

2
A Biblical Warning: "Don't Rejoice Panama"

by the Popular Christian Movement in Panama[8]

> *Woe to the man who builds a town*
> *on blood and founds a city on iniquity.*
> Habakkuk 2:12

On Dec. 23, 1989, Dr. Arias Calderon (one of U.S.-designated vice-presidents) stated that he and the other new leaders of Panama had not requested the invasion by the U.S. Army and only had knowledge of the imperialist plan hours before it occurred. This is one more lie presented to our people at the very moment the massacre was being carried out by the imperial mercenaries. These three leaders—Calderon, Endara and Ford—took possession of their new posts at the headquarters of the Southern Command and now they intend to wash off the Panamanian blood which served to legitimize their coming to power, fulfilling their thirst for power. What kind of men are these?

What kind of leaders? What class of rulers will Endara, Calderon and Ford be? Men who yearn for power! A yearning which made them accomplices in this massacre. Because the guilty are not only those mercenaries who fired against our people but also this genocidal and puppet government which legitimized that massacre.

For these new governors, it was easier and more comfortable to take power through the help of the North American army rather than through the Panamanian people, making us believe that we are cowards and irresponsible. What governor can govern who doesn't believe in his own people? It is very easy (for the government) to ask for reconciliation when one hasn't lost a friend, brother or family member, while at the same time a river of blood was flowing in Panama. Thousands of Panamanians have fallen, HEROS and MARTYRS, who demand justice of these executioners and of the Yankee who once again has usurped our territory. As the Bible says,

> Don't rejoice, Philistine nation, that the rod of the one who punished you has been broken (Noriega), because from the asp from which that serpent came forth will now come forth a viper, and even more, a flying dragon (U.S.A.)—Is.14:29

The president of the United States along with his local puppets has taken advantage of the people's yearning for justice and liberty, hiding the data about the dead and wounded while bombing El Chorrillo and other barrios. The media, controlled by the Southern Command, said: "Everything is under control; there is no resistance." Later, authorized U.S.spokesmen admitted their surprise at *the courage and fury with which the Dignity Battalions and CODEPADIs resisted.*[9] With little preparation in facing this, the most powerful army in the continent, indeed, one of the most powerful in the world, the Dignity Battalions and Codepadis resisted. The generous blood offered up to the nation by our heros and martyrs has been transformed into the fertile seed from which a *national liberation* will rise.

Notes

Editors Note: The drug role of these three colonial leaders totally contradicts the propaganda that it was Noriega's drug dealing that forced the invasion (see p. 171).

1. Cristobal Arboleda Alfaro, "Contra Quien Guerreamos?" *Opinion Publica*, Nov., 1989, No. 22, p. 12.

2. Ibid.

3. The "13th month" or Christmas bonus is a common practice in many Latin American countries, paid either by the government or private employers, a form of charity because of hard times or low pay, so families can have some Christmas.

4. Gregorio Selser, *Panama:Erase Un Pais a Un Canal Pegado*, Universidad Obrera de Mexico, D.F., 1989.

5. Jose E. Stoute, "Las Leyes de la Guerra," *Opinion Publica*, Nov. 1989, No. 22, p. 4.

6. The famous 1964 Flag Riots which precipitated the entire process of Panama's struggle for sovereignty.

7. Gregorio Selser, *Panama: Erase Un Pais a Un Canal Pegado*, op. cit., p. 112.

8. Movimiento Popular Cristiana (MPC), "Camilo Torres Restrepo," a reflection paper issued in Panama, Feb. 1, 1990.

9. Note: CODEPADIs were emergency Committees for the Defense of the Nation organized at the neighborhood level.

PART I

INSIDE PANAMA: TOTAL WAR—
ITS HUMAN & POLITICAL IMPACT

The U.S. Army employed a new model of aggression in Panama:
total war. The object was to destroy and annihilate the enemy
with a minimum of losses to U.S. troops. Low intensity
warfare has been surpassed by the Pentagon with
the experience of this invasion.[10]

—Raul Marin, special reporter

Bombed out apartment buildings in El Chorrillo destroyed by U.S. forces in
their aerial attacks on the headquarters of the Panamanian Defense Forces,
Dec. 21, 1989.

IMPACT OF TOTAL WAR ON THE PANAMANIAN NATION

1
The Destruction of El Chorrillo

from *Opinion Publica*[11]

The city of Panama exploded at 12:45 A.M. on December 20, 1989. Tremendous explosions and huge flames began to rise from one of the most populated barrios of the capital, El Chorrillo. The U.S. army will not provide data about the intensity of the weapons-fire employed in this operation. The survivors were enclosed in refugee camps and after about four days of this "humanitarian attention" they all repeated the same story: the bodies of members of the Dignity Battalions loyal to the government had been incinerated in houses and cars as victims of the U.S. attack. According to official figures, the attack on the general headquarters of the Panamanian Defense Forces (FDP) left 80 civilians dead. U.S. announcers claimed that a majority of these died as a result of fires started by troops loyal to Noriega. Panamanian observers tell a different story:

> The reverberations of explosions and detonations began in our nation during the early morning of December 20th, 1989. All this activity occurring within the perimeter of the capital city against specific objectives as recorded by one of our instruments, a unit that is part of a larger future national seismo-

graphic network, although it is not connected to the worldwide instrument system of WWSSN. This unit recorded 417 explosions during the first 14 hours of December 20 ... in El Chorrillo.[10]

From December 20 onward, some 14,000 persons were left homeless as a result of the bombing visited upon El Chorrillo barrio as part of the U.S. attacks. The bombs destroyed approximately 3,983 homes, located around the Central Headquarters of the FDP.

Census data shows that 14,170 persons lived in the sectors of the barrio that were destroyed. Of that population, 40% were minors 14 years and under. Of all the housing there, only 12% was considered as "owned" by residents, whereas 46.5% was "ceded" and 41.3% was rented at an average of $18 per month. These characteristics of this barrio should not be forgotten when preparing programs of social assistance.

According to information from the newspapers, the 2,400 families that were victims of the El Chorrillo bombings, were taken to U.S. Army camps where they were subject to very strict regulations. Everyone was registered and no one was allowed outside the camp except between 6 A.M. and 8 P.M.

2
Flame Throwers Burn Bodies in Cocle

from CODEHUCA, Doc. #2

The fatalities from the bombings in this province alone vary from between 700 and 800, civilians and military. Those reporting on the dead also mention the use of torture by the U.S. military against certain prisoners of war, in particular those soldiers from the Defense Forces called "Machos del Monte."

Medical personnel who provided attention to the wounded indicate that the U.S. Army utilized new, experimental weapons during the invasion. They noticed that some people were wounded with a type of weapon that practically put a hole through their victims which produced profuse hemorrhaging, as from a colander. Since these medical personnel had no medicine or resources to deal with this type of wound, many of the wounded bled to death. . . .

We also know that the U.S. Army carried out "sanitation" activities in which they used *flamethrowers to burn hundreds of bodies*. They also used *common graves* in which they buried hundreds of bodies. These last activities are linked to the rumors of "disappearances," reflecting the discrepancy between the numbers of missing persons and the lists of prisoners.

In early January 1990, Base Christian Communities (Catholic religious groups) from Darien, Colon and Comarca de San Blas provinces published a denunciation in the *Panama Star*, in which they informed the public of the obstacles they encountered when trying to find out the exact number of dead. According to their lowest calculations, no less than 3,000 Panamanians were killed in the invasion.

Regarding their reference to torture, one "Macho del Monte" soldier reported that a wound on his lower leg was caused by a projectile which lodged in the sole of his foot. U.S. soldiers took a metal cable (such as that used to hang up laundry) and introduced it into the hole until it touched the projectile producing intense pain. Another Macho del Monte soldier was hung up by one arm on which he already had an injury to his elbow, though that wound had been stitched up.[12]

3
Implosion at Coco Solo, Colon

from *Pensamiento Propio*

At the headquarters of the Defense Forces at Coco Solo, Colon—the second largest city in the country—one can hardly see any remains from the battle. The headquarters is intact with only a few smoke stains around its main windows. There isn't a single explosion hole in the facade, yet the 300 Panamanian soldiers who were inside died there without a single U.S. soldier losing his life. The explanation for this unusual phenomenon is that a bomb landed inside the building with such force that it caused the building to "implode" instantly killing everyone inside.

The headquarters building at Coco Solo was destroyed during the early hours of Dec. 20th. By dawn, helicopters were flying over the city looking for any sign of resistance. When an armed gunman fired at U.S. soldiers from a multi-family apartment building, immediately two missiles were launched at the building. The explosions shook the whole city of Colon. The first exploded the whole section of the building where the rifleman had been, while the second went through the building and exploded in the dining room of a nearby house. Three days later, when the U.S. infantry arrived, people ran out into the street to greet them and denounce Noriega's followers.[13]

The official figures (from the Southern Command) claimed that only 60 persons died in Colon, 40 of these civilians, but neither the humanitarian organizations nor the churches accept that count and claim no less than 300 deaths. Witnesses described how bodies were disposed of: they were placed in plastic bags and put into refrigerated trucks (container trailers from the Free Zone in Colon) because of lack of space in the morgue. For the United States, this constituted a "clean operation" because not a single U.S. soldier was killed.

4
Pacora Bombed With Chemical Substances

from *El Periodico*

One of the few reports concerning U.S. attacks on places in the interior of the country came from the semi-mountainous village of Pacora, near Panama City. The village was bombed with chemical substances by helicopters and aircraft from the Southern Command. Various persons who live there appealed to human rights organizations and press media to denounce this brutal form of warfare by the Army of the South (Southern Command).

Other residents affirmed that this chemical substance burned their skin, producing intense stinging and diarrhea. They also fear the substance may affect their health in other ways. The people of Pacora also declared that their town was converted into a huge concentration camp surrounded by barbed wire, as the Nazis used to do, so that its inhabitants couldn't offer any assistance to the Panamanian soldiers who were camped in the mountainous region nearby at the time of the U.S. invasion of Panama.[14]

5
Panama: Testing Ground for New U.S. Weapons

Reuters, Jan. 9, 1990

U.S. military leaders are proud of the demonstration of their new weapons and techniques used during the Panama invasion, ranging from 500-foot parachute jumps to high-tech apparatus for night vision.

High-level Pentagon officials in Washington, D.C. told *Reuters* that the new and expensive military equipment functioned better than expected in the night attack on Dec. 20th, whose objective was to end the regime of strongman Manuel Antonio Noriega. . . .

The new weapons included the use of the super-secret "stealth" attack-bomber in combat for the first time, with its anti-radar devices. They included also the Apache helicopters, a new "Jeep" and the latest in bullet-proof jackets and helmets. Communications, the vital element in modern warfare, showed great improvement, they said. "I know that Grenada was a nightmare in terms of communications," said one high-level officer from the U.S. air force in relation to the attack on that Caribbean island in 1983. They talked a lot at that time about how U.S. troops had to use public telephones to ask for support when their military communications failed. "But clearly that was not the case in Panama," the officer said, asking not to be identified. "The Army could speak to us and we with them." Another officer, Lt. Gen. Jimmy Ross, Chief Assistant to the Army High Command for logistical matters, stated that thousands of air-transport troops and "Rangers" jumped from 500 foot altitudes out of the doors of heavy C-141 and C-130 transport planes, and relatively speaking, there were few accidents.

These Army officers, explaining these surprise jumps, stated that shortly after midnight on Dec. 20th during the house-to-house combat over the next 48 hours, new, sophisticated weapons as well as the overwhelming numbers of U.S. troops involved (up to 25,000 soldiers) had a lot to do with pulling Panamanian troops loyal to Noriega out of hiding. In the battle, they used eleven new Apache attack helicopters (AH-64)—built by the McDonnell Douglass Corporation—each costing $14 million. The Apache helicopters replace the Cobra AH-l from the Vietnam era and they didn't lose a single one. "Our great success was due to them having night vision systems," said Ross, referring to equipment which costs $1 million per unit and allows the pilot to see as if it were daylight.

The Apache helicopter, designed to destroy tanks of the Warsaw Pact armies in Europe, used hellfire missiles and 30mm rapid-fire cannons to finish off the Panamanian troops before dawn. Ross said he spoke with the pilots who used this system: Apaches can suspend in the air, observe from more or less 1,000 meters, watch U.S. troops when they enter a residential area and observe where the enemy exits.

The military officers also praised the HMMWV (high mobility multiple use rotating vehicle) because of its strength. They said that even such heavy equipment as the HMMWV was launched by parachute from only 1,100 foot altitudes, just prior to the paratroopers touching ground. Gen. Ross underscored the fact that "One of these HMMWV landed upside down and turned itself upright . . . when the Panamanian troops saw that, they turned and distanced themselves from it."

The most exotic weapon in the invasion was the F-117A "stealth" bomber which made its debut in combat in Panama. At least one of these attack aircraft with swept-back wings flew to Panama from its desert base in Tonopah, Nevada (USA) to command an attack on the FDP base in Rio Hato where it fired two 2,000 pound bombs to stun and disorient Noriega's troops. . . . [15]

6
Thesis of Total War

Philip E. Wheaton

In addition to the massive onslaught by the U.S. forces, totally out-manning and over-powering the relatively weaker and numerically smaller FDP troops, there were several unique aspects about this invasion that argue in favor of a calculated strategy that had little to do with Panama itself. The most obvious is that Noriega could have easily been killed or kidnapped any time U.S. agencies or agents might have decided to do so. Equally obvious is the fact that many FDP officers were sympathetic to the United States and held no anti-American animosities or progressive ideological positions for which they were ready to sacrifice their lives. In other words, it would have been easy for the Southern Command to have occupied Panama without using such destructive methods as attacking a civilian population, especially at midnight when it was asleep and totally unprepared to defend itself, unless the Pentagon had an entirely different rationale for the invasion, such as to practice an attack of this kind with new equipment under combat conditions: *total war*.

The term "total war" refers to a carefully planned, surgical military operation designed to destroy or so debilitate any resistance that the battle will be over *in a very short time*. In contrast to Vietnam or the low intensity war fought in El Salvador over the past decade, *total war* is aimed at quickly destroying all opposition within a few hours or days. Therefore, it is the polar opposite of protracted warfare and for that very reason, must be massive or "total" in nature. This kind of warfare is also *total* in the sense that the U.S. forces exercize complete control over all aspects of civilian life, such as: reporting on the war by foreign reporters and the national media, the policies of the puppet or sympathetic local government leaders, all communications and movement by civilians, occupation of all highways, electric power centers and radio stations. Most importantly, it exercizes psychological control over both the domestic population (in the US) and the target population (in Panama).

In the case of the Panamanian invasion, some 120 psychological warfare experts were used to handle every human, social and political aspect of control after the takeover by the combat troops. This included: interrogating prisoners, arresting and questioning potential political opposition leaders, responding to human rights inquiries, and conditioning the two primary civilian populations. For instance, the North American population was never shown the victim population, as the Panamanian dead were quickly buried and thus hidden from public view. The Panamanian population was forcibly kept indoors or terrorized on the streets, as well as being isolated from the burial process and the political prisoners. So it was days before most

Panamanians learned details of the invasion, thus keeping their emotional response to a minimum. In the case of North American families, this "limited" loss of life meant we could leave our television sets and get on with our Christmas meal. While Panamanians had no traditional Christmas in 1989, many did get some Christmas presents from the massive looting. Strong evidence—to be detailed later— suggests that the looting was intentional and even encouraged by the U.S. occupation forces in order to compensate the looters psychologically for their otherwise disastrous Yuletide.

The thesis of "total war" will be developed further as we proceed. At this point, it is clear that the invasion was meticulously planned and that it served a purpose similar to Hitler's war on Spain where he tested the German weapons of war—like dive-bombers—which would be used in WWII. In the case of the U.S. invasion of Panama, the Pentagon was experimenting with this total war model for use against other Third World countries, when conditions and circumstances permit, as in the Gulf war against Iraq.

7
"We No Longer Have A Nation"

Dr. Mauro Zuniga

Dr. Zuniga, a popular civic leader described the state of Panama soon after the invasion in these strong words: "From December 20th on, we no longer have a nation.... In an attack without precedent in military history, the United States has levelled the defenses of the Panamanian army and in less than four days that institution lays in ruin. The U.S. Army trained and guided the Defense Forces in such a way that when they decided to unleash their fury, they knew exactly where to strike. During the early morning hours of Dec. 20th, they pulverized the three military bases of the FDP in the metropolitan area ....

"However, this massive destruction by the U.S. invasion forces is not any reason to abandon the task of beginning to rebuild our nation immediately. During this new period, the struggle will be for us Panamanians to define what we intend this nation to be...."[16]

Mortal Cry

Norah de Alba
December 22, 1989

This poem by Norah de Alba is the earliest known poetic response to the U.S. invasion reflecting the suffering and protest of the Panamanian people —ED.

They arrived
as do thieves in the shadows
—imperceptibly—
In complicity with our sleep.

They arrived,
and broke the silence of the stars
—from ocean to ocean—
with steel and screams they cut the
early morning hours of our streets
breaking the night in two
carving up the dawn,
the nature of their way.

They arrived
with complete arrogance
drugged with a sense of power
on the winds of their filibustering.

They arrived and sounded
their trumpets in the Isthmus
arriving with their tanks and bullets
with reporters from the UPI
and their cans of processed food.

They arrived
and said—casually—
that they had come in the name

of peace to make war;
that they were coming to "democratize"
the people, to wipe clean
with cannon blasts
at the price of blood, pain and fear;
said they had come to impose
"national justice"
through genocide.

They went on invading us
In the name of that "liberty"!
In the name of that "liberty"
their tanks fired on us!
In the name of such a "democracy"
they raised their little flags!
In the name of such "justice"
they climbed into their helicopters
and bombed our houses
and streets;
our barrios
and children;
our pregnant women
and old people;
our youth
and civilian population
and our military partiots . . . !

They arrived
as they have always come to Our America
—in their north american way—
to kill Panamanians! (17)

Translated by Philip Wheaton

Notes

9. *Pensamiento Propio*, CRIES, Managua, Nicaragua, No. 67, Jan/Feb 1990, p. 28
10. *Liberacion*, MLN-29-XI, Panama, Feb. 1990, Universidad de Panama p. 19.
11. *Opinion Publica*, CELA, Panama, No. 24, Feb. 1990, Magela Cabrera Arias,

"La Reconstruccion in El Chorrillo," pp. 8-9.

12. CODEHUCA, Testimonies recorded by staff of the Central American Human Rights Committees, San Jose, Costa Rica, taken in Panama, Jan. 29, 1990 from Fernando Araujo, Red Cross contact.

13. *Pensamiento Propio*, Jan/Feb 1990, op. cit., "La guerra total de Bush," p. 28.

14. *El Periodico*, "Bombardean Pacora con substsancias quimicas," Panama, Occupied Territory, Feb 1990, p. 8.

15. *Reuters*, Washington, D.C., Jan. 9, 1990, published in *Tropic Times*.

16. Dr. Mauro Zuniga, "Ejercito norteamericano ocupa todo el territorio de la Republica," *Opinion Publica*, No. 24, op. cit., p. 3.

17. *El Periodico*, "Panama, Occupied Territory," Feb. 1990, p. 3.

HUMAN SUFFERING AND SOCIAL COSTS
OF THE U.S. INVASION

*"With immense pain we find ourselves living
today in an invaded country"*
—Pro-Independence Popular Sectors

8
The Magnitude of the Suffering &
"Dance of the Numbers"

The magnitude of the U.S. invasion can best be appreciated in terms of its human impact on the Panamanian society, as measured by the number of deaths and degree of human suffering. There are various versions of data but countering all the official figures, especially those given out by the Southern Command, the passage of time and eye-witness reports indicate a much larger number of deaths, wounded and homeless. This so-called "dance of the numbers" is due not so much to more or less accurate figures, but to the political intention of those in charge who wanted to portray the suffering and dying as far smaller than the facts have subsequently proven. In reviewing this data, the number of political prisoners and those left homeless are equally important indicators of the damage done to the Panamanian people by the the U.S. invaders.

The official military and governmental sources offer extremely low figures, all of which data is controlled by the Southern Command:

- Southern Command: 300 military and 250 civilian dead
- Panamanian Human Rights: confirms 207 civilian dead
- Panamanian Red Cross: 200 dead, no details.

By contrast, those present on the scene, private legal and non-governmental humanitarian groups, families of those who have lost loved ones, and first hand medical witnesses present figures ten times as high:

- *Ramsey Clark*, ex-U.S. Attorney General: "more than 1,000 dead and possibly multiples of thousands (i.e., 2-3,000)."
- *Panamanian Doctors to CODEHUCA*: at least five mass graves with dozens of bodies in each, plus 3 container trailers with some hundreds in each potentially, plus 700-800 claimed in Cocle province alone. By May 1990, the number of common graves had risen to 14 confirmed.
- *Pro-Democratic Panamanians* (New York City):
  Up to 2,000 dead (many buried in clandestine graves)
  6,000 wounded, including military and civilians
  7,000 political prisoners held incommunicado
  15,000 left homeless (figure verified in El Chorrillo)

In light of the difficulty in obtaining complete or accurate data from official sources, including the Southern Command, this "dance of the numbers" continues. Part of the confusion arises from the difficulty of determining if those reported "disappeared" died as a result of the invasion, whether they have been detained or are incommunicado in Southern Command camps, or whether some of these persons may have hidden themselves or are still resisting the occupation forces.

Nonetheless, as we get further away from the time of the invasion itself, and even though the numbers of the dead and wounded continue to grow, we may never know the actual figures. The information coming in suggests, however, that the number of dead is far greater than the figures officially cited.[18]

9
Testimonies From First-Hand Witnesses

The following testimonies are taken from original docu-
ments provided by the Central American Human Rights
Center (CODEHUCA) and the Panamanian Human
Rights Organization (CONADEHUPA)[19]

Case No. 1 Undertaker at Amador Cemetery

He recovered 200 corpses from the Central Headquarters (FDP).
The bodies were in a decomposed state and many still in their
underwear. U.S. soldiers paid him $6 for each body!

Case No. 2 Journalism Student

He left Santo Tomas hospital for the Jardin de Paz cemetery. That
afternoon a truckload of bombed bodies left the morgue of the
hospital with 28 bodies to be buried in a common grave at this
cemetery. Personnel from the Public Ministry (Procurador General)
were present, including Ana Belfon, a public prosecutor.

On the same day, in the presence of these functionaries and some
families of the disappeared, neighbors watched as the U.S. soldiers
displayed 29 plastic bags (military green color) which appeared to
contain more than one body in each case, for the bodies were
destroyed and in a decomposed state. Then the bodies recognized by
their families along with those unidentified were buried in the
common grave. The bodies were placed crosswise, the width of the
grave, filling approximately a quarter of the in this manner.

Case No. 5 Man Wounded By Machine-Gun Fire

On Dec. 20th, a man was travelling along the Inter-American
Highway between Chorrera and Arraijan in a private automobile when
it was intercepted by a U.S. tank and a Hummer vehicle (new style
heavy-armored jeep). The driver stopped, the passengers assuming it
was a routine check, but were surprised by a grenade explosion and

a shot from the tank which killed two of the people, Rubina Gonzalez and Jose Espinosa and wounding two others, Osvaldo Polo and Camilo Chen. After the explosion, the soldiers left and they drove the car (on flat tires) to the Nicolas Solano Hospital where they received medical attention.

Case No. 6 Wounded Person Still Hospitalized

At 1 A.M. on the morning of Dec. 20th, he was riding on a bus on Panama-Chorrera route when it was attacked by a U.S. tank. Twenty-six persons on board died.

Case No. 7 Panamanian Doctor Reports on Common Graves

On Dec. 23rd, a doctor was moved to a concentration camp at Emperador to attend to the wounded detained there. About 30 persons had gunshot wounds and burns requiring hospitalization. The fact that the rural facilities were inadequate was communicated to U.S. personnel and a move was initiated. But because of the late hour, the wounded had to sleep in the camp. In conversation with U.S. paramedics, he was told that there was a common grave where they had buried three trailers-full of bodies. Witnesses have verified that there are such refrigerated trailers in the city. The paramedics indicated that each trailer could hold 400 bodies. Similarly, they mentioned the cremations at El Chorrillo, indicating that such an act was justified because of the advanced state of decomposition of the bodies.

Case No. 8 Manual laborer at the University of Panama

On Dec. 22, a manual laborer went to the Central Headquarters with a group of people who had seen U.S. soldiers take some bodies from among the debris. Near the chapel, one of the U.S. soldiers was using a flamethrower to burn a body. The apparatus was held on their backs, having a hose and what looked like a ventilator. The bodies were placed on top of a piece of zinc. When the fire went out, the body was like a piece of coal—a compact mass—which was then put into a green bag that had three adjustable straps. After that body was burned, it was placed together with others which had already been cremated.

One thing that caught his attention was the reaction of a woman who was shouting that they shouldn't do this because the families then couldn't identify the bodies. But the soldiers didn't stop as no one was around to identify the bodies. Nor did they photograph the bodies for later identification.

Case No. 9 Doctor Receives U.S. Ultimatum

On Dec. 22, a Panamanian doctor received an ultimatum from the U.S. Army through the Red Cross that if we didn't let them enter the hospital, it would be bombed. So we allowed them to enter. They searched the hospital for weapons but found none. In the morgue were 60 bodies which they stabbed to make sure they were all dead. (19)

Case No. 10 Mother's Testimony of Being Caught In the Bombing at San Miguelito

I lived through that day of Dec. 20th as if it were years of anguish. As soon as we realized that they were bombing the city, we got out of bed and I went to collect water.

In the morning, I went to where my daughter was and I saw the helicopter there. After a few soldiers had gotten on board, it climbed up into the air and shortly after they started to fire their weapons.

I gathered the children and my son his nephews because of the missile that landed in my daughter's bedroom. She is now hospitalized. At that moment, as my son was putting the children under the bed, we saw the bomb fall. I threw myself into my bedroom. I heard my son scream, come out and yell: "Mama!" I saw him bathed in blood. We still have blood on the walls.

Right then, I went out as my youngest child called me: "Mama, Mama!" I answered: "My child." She said, "I am injured." Then I saw that I too was covered with blood and that my arm was injured. I stopped looking for my other children because they weren't there. When I entered the bedroom, I saw my youngest child on the floor, the one who is now hospitalized. "My child," I screamed. "Mama,

I left to go to the kitchen to look for my husband. I saw him bathed in blood and started to scream: "They killed my husband; they killed my children!"

Well, then my two grandchildren came in, my daughter's daughters. They came down when they saw my husband, became nervous and started to scream: "Papa, Papa." I screamed because I saw him leave. When I went outside ... Alexis had grabbed his brother because he tried to throw himself over the wall, so he grabbed him and pulled him down and then fainted. Since then I don't what became of them.

When he went down there, the men took a shortcut across the walk. When he reached it he fainted, falling with his brother who turned and lifted him up. When they arrived, he was unconscious.

When my daughter and her husband brought us down from the house, I went out screaming. I don't know how I got there but they took care of us right away and got us to safety.

This experience is something I will never forget my whole life, as long as I live, while I exist. Because of what has happened, whenever I hear a helicopter, I'm afraid. Last night I couldn't sleep because early in the evening they started flying over the area.[20]

Case No. 11 Two Young Men See U.S. Soldiers Burning Houses

On the night of Dec. 19th, we began to hear some shots during the evening. When I was going to bed about 11:30 P.M., I heard a powerful noise that caused the building to shake. Later, I learned that it was a huge U.S. air force jet. The bombardments began immediately after the plane passed overhead.

I shouted to my wife and children to get down on the floor. We heard and felt the bombs and machine gun strafing all around the building. Instantly, all the windows in our apartment were broken, with things falling from the roof and windows, so we went into the bathroom and crouched down on the floor all night.

At sunrise, it was calmer so we went downstairs and outside. On the way down, we saw total destruction—doors and support beams blown out. We talked with our neighbors who had also crouched in fear all night as we had. Many told us of bullets and projectiles passing through their walls. A personal friend of mine was hit by a passing through their walls. A personal friend of mine was hit by a bullet in the foot while in his bed.

Before reaching the street, we saw a group of some 18 U.S. soldiers coming down the street. We saw them entering each house and the residents coming out followed by the soldiers and then we saw the houses, one by one, going up in smoke. *The U.S. soldiers were burning our houses!*

Some of the people were trapped in their apartments because they lived on the second floors of these wooden houses because the stairs down to the ground floor were already on fire, so that many people had to jump from the balconies....

So, to repeat, I do not think the people in the houses knew the soldiers were going to burn them, because otherwise they would have left before. But the people were terrified with the troops in the streets; the people were very afraid of them.

Leaving the building, we saw some 8 bodies inside the building in the stairway leading down to the first floor.... In the street, we saw bodies strewn on the road. I think they might have been people who fled during the night, scared, and were shot down by U.S. troops.... I cannot say how they died, only that they were dead. In the street, it was clear that most had died from bullet wounds.[21]

Case No.12. Doctor: More About the Common Graves

I work in the ———— Hospital and on Saturday, Dec. 23rd, the director of our hospital was called and told that the "common graves" *(fosas comunes)* were going to be dug on hospital property. The director was completely opposed to this idea, because—as he said—there was no reason to discriminate against the patients of his hospital just because they were considered to be "crazy."

The plan was to keep the patients inside their rooms and then to dig the pit.... It was the Minister of Health, Dr. Triny Castillero, who had given the order about the common grave, but my director—who has since been removed from his post—said that he needed legal authorization to do something like that, so he did not allow it. He denied the permission even when the government argued that in times of war, all land reverts to its domain.

As it turned out, whether because of the patients or for other reasons, they did not dig the pits on our hospital property. Rather, they dug them elsewhere. For example, we were told that a number of the dead (who died as a result of some fighting that took place behind the Municipal Hospital) were taken to the Jardin de Paz—the Peace Garden—and buried there in a common grave.

We were also told that a numbers of cadavers from El Chorrillo had been buried in a common grave at El Amador. I have not gone to visit these places. Also, behind the Municipal Cemetery of Juan Dia, I was told that after a serious exchange of gunfire one night during the invasion, there was a high number of deaths and that a pit had been dug there.

Normally, only unidentifiable bodies should be put into common graves. While I do not know of many cases personally, I do know that some of those bodies put into common graves could have been identified. In one case, they buried a cadaver that had full identification on it. Your delegation should try to speak with some of the family members. So, yes, they have buried persons who could have been identified, along with numerous unidentifiable bodies. I think they did this, in part, *so that the real number of the dead would not be known*.

I came to this conclusion because during the first days of the invasion when I was working in the hospital, U.S. troops were not giving access to the bodies to persons looking for family members. I personally tried to help when I could by taking photos of the bodies for those who came looking. I would go and check the bodies myself.[22]

10
How Much Is Life Worth In Panama?

by Javier Perez

In this world, there are many things that don't seem to have clear answers, although as a result of the advances in technology, very few. Now one of the irreparable things in this world is human life, perhaps because it is the only thing—according to some—of value, even though others affirm it's worth nothing. With everything that has happened around this invasion, what we mainly lost were human lives. But for General Marc Cisneros (U.S. Southern Command chief) Panamanian lives don't seem to be worth anything.

What is certain in all this tragedy is that businessmen to the right and left have been coming forth to claim indemnification, alleging that they lost some $2 billion from the bombing and looting. The United States has refused to pay for these damages claiming that it was Noriega's fault and that he should pay, and furthermore, that all the United States did was to intervene for a "just cause," although so far no one has been able to ascertain for whom this invasion was just.

On the other hand, we know that this "just" invasion cost the lives of at least 7,000 Panamanians and that is what pains us so deeply. If the military action by the gringos was just and their cause too, then certainly it would be just to pay the families of those thousands who died in the invasion some indemnification. But strangely, neither the gringos nor the leaders of this colony have demanded any such payment from the Bush administration for these deaths.

So one thing remains clear: in Panama, life isn't worth anything, because the families of the victims haven't received even enough with which to bury their dead ones properly; indeed, thousands were buried in common graves, which represents an olympian deprecation of both human life and death. So here in Panama, life isn't worth anything. Nor do we understand why people are waiting around and not demanding such indemnification, for it is clear they were not killed by the dictator but by the invasion forces.

Obviously, the authorities of this "democracy" in the exercise of "social justice" have the last word, but they had better be CAREFUL with these dead, for one day they will arise and demand JUSTICE![23]

Notes

18. *Opinion Publica*, Feb 1990, op. cit., Giancarlo Soler, "Los Muertos Provocados Por La Invasion," pp. 6-7.
19-22.CODEHUCA (Central American Human Rights Committee), Testimonies gathered by staff in Jan. 1990, Panama. Office in San Jose, Costa Rica, subsequently summarized in *Brecha*, a Joint Report of CODEHUCA/CONADEHUPA, Jan-Feb. 1990, No. 6, San Jose, Costa Rica.
23. Javier Perez, "Cuanto Vale La Vida En Panama?," *El Periodico*, Feb. 1990, p. 4.

One of several common graves created by U.S. forces to mass bury Panamanians killed in the invasion of Dec. 1989.

PSYCHOLOGICAL WARFARE: CREATE A WALL OF SILENCE AND CLEAN UP THE MESS

11
A Wall of Silence Exists Here

Ramsey Clark

On January 5, 1990, General Marc Cisneros (Chief of the Southern Command) declared to the international press that "This action will pass into history as a positive effort." But that same day, Ramsey Clark, ex-Attorney General of the United States, checked hospitals and morgues in the Panamanian capital trying without success to obtain reliable data on the number of victims. By contrast, he declared that "A wall of silence exists here. They are trying to cover up the human cost of this operation." Ramsey Clark should know, for he was the lawyer who defended Eugene Hausenfus in 1986.

Ramsey Clark doesn't believe that the number of civilian dead can be less than 1,500 even though the Pentagon talks of only 350. After visiting El Chorrillo, the ex-judge affirmed that "it looked like a desert." He arrived when bulldozers of the U.S. army had already begun to remove the ruins. For three days, no one could enter the barrio because soldiers were removing the cadavers and wiping out the signs of their action. The wall of silence around the damages of that initial devastating attack was handled with the same efficiency as the missiles that perforated the walls of the army headquarters.[24]

12
"No Comment" from the Southern Command

Waiting for nine days in front of the Apostolic Nunciatura where
Noriega had taken refuge, few foreign reporters were interested in the
common graves of the Panamanian dead. Even most Panamanian
reporters refused to investigate the matter, indeed, most of what we
know about their deaths has come from anonymous sources. The new
government installed an information office to coordinate information
on victims. Located in front of the National Headquarters for Investigations, at the entrance to one of the central posts of the Southern
Command, few people darkened its doors. Capt. Maritza Palm—ex-
member of the old Defense Forces—now incorporated into the Public
Force—spoke with irritation in her voice: "We only give out information to the families of those affected. This is individual data. We're
not going to give them any overall list." There was no telephone in
her office and all business was done in person.

Capt. Skalton—director of one of the prisoner camps—was also
irritated about showing any list of detainees, even though at least
5,000 prisoners passed through his camp. All were interrogated by
U.S. military police or Pentagon intelligence personnel. In the
corridors where these interrogations took place, computers functioned
day and night, with the same efficiency with which the gringos set up
105 tents and stretched out 780 rolls of barbed wire. According to
Skalton, 2,500 prisoners were still being detained, 1,500 had been re-
integrated into the new Public Force, and the remainder were
transferred to refugee camps.

Capt. Skalton assured us that the prisoners' human rights were
respected according to the Geneva Convention accords, although he
added that this conflict did not constitute a state of war. "The prisoners still cannot receive visits from family members and lawyers, but
they do receive legal assistance from AID and we are advising their
families through the Panamanian mails." Of course, the post office
stopped operating from the outset of the invasion and the press was
not allowed near the barbed-wire fence where the prisoners are. But

some greeted us with a raised fist or the victory sign.

Many of these prisoners' names appear on a list which a reactionary group began to draw up in 1987, while other prisoners saw their names on the pages of the daily newspaper *El Siglo* which had just reappeared in print. On Dec. 29, 1989, this newspaper published a list of "drug addicts" in which the names of politicians and businessmen appeared, persons linked to the government since 1968. The article said: "These subjects must not be allowed to escape for any reason." When some citizens protested, *El Siglo* confirmed the fact that this list had been provided by the *U.S intelligence service*. In any case, the witch hunt had already begun.[25]

13
The Southern Command Holds Total Control Over Panama

Cecilio E. Simon E., Dean, University of Panama

> *Following is a list of twelve aspects of the U.S. control over Panama and cover-up of the invasion, including: control of victim information, political prisoners and control of the media. This official report from the Dean of the Faculty of Public Administration, Cecilio E. Simon E., of the University of Panama was sent to the Martin Luther King, Jr. Convention on Human Rights, Jan. 13, 1990.*

[T]he following facts represent a brief review of the situation:

- Iron-fisted control over the entire country by the U.S. Army which prevents any Panamanian institution from investigating actual casualties caused by the invasion;
- Figures of the dead, wounded and disappeared are kept in strict confidence, while clearly altered reports are provided by the Southern Command;
- The public has not been informed about the locations of common graves or concentration camps so that family members can discover the whereabouts of disappeared family

members;

- Access to hospitals and public offices which might provide information regarding disappeared civilians is controlled by the U.S. Army;
- The incineration of bodies on the beaches near El Chorrillo by U.S. military troops, a fact confirmed by testimonies of residents of the area, was kept secret;
- The detention of civilians who oppose the occupation without arrest orders issued by Panamanian civil authorities. Anonymous denunciations used as a basis for such civilian arrests;
- All information regarding detention has been denied, justice tribunals are not working and the protection of *habeus corpus* and constitutional guarantees are not respected;
- Detention of persons in concentration camps incommunicado without access to them by their family members. Prisoners of war kept outside in the sun and rain and hand-cuffed for hours as a form of torture;
- Media control has been exercised by the occupation forces. News announcers' texts are prepared by the Public Affairs Office of the Southern Command which acts as a censor;
- The dismissal of everyone who opposes the current regime from governmental jobs; union leaders have been detained in order to pressure them to support the puppet government;
- Residences and offices of political groups which oppose the invasion have been searched and in many cases their files have been destroyed and valuables stolen. Political leaders in opposition to the government have received threats they will be detained;
- Members of the Public Force (new military/police organization) are responsible only to the orders of the U.S. Southern Command, and their identification cards are signed by General Maxwell Thurman. They are thus accredited to move through the national territory of the Republic of Panama to aid the U.S. Army.

Friends, the above statement in no way constitutes an exhaustive list of the atrocities committed by the U.S. government through their occupation forces. With the help of those who recognize the legacy of the Founding Fathers of the great nation to the North and who support the fight for civil rights led by Martin Luther King, Jr., we will move ahead.

Reiterating the greetings of thousands of patriotic Panamanians who hope your deliberations will help our suffering nation, I conclude this letter.

Sincerely yours,

CECILIO E. SIMON E., Dean
Faculty of Public Administration[26]

14
U.S. Clean-up Operation: "Kill Anything That Moves"

Maruya Torres, Spanish reporter

"When the U.S. tanks became aware that we were there, they turned and began to fire on us. Nobody other than us reporters were on the street. No sharpshooters or Panamanian forces, only us reporters, my chauffeur and assistant were under our car, terrorized, praying."

Maruya Torres is a Spanish reporter from the prestigious Madrid daily *El Pais* and was in Panama at the time of the U.S. military invasion, an assignment which cost the life of her work companion, Juan Antonio Rodriguez, a photographer.

"They fired 50 mm bullets at us which when they hit sprayed out shrapnel along with the bullets. One of these bullets penetrated the left eye of my companion, Juantxu, which then passed through his skull and out his right ear, causing his death (as we learned later)."

Just before he was hit, two U.S. tanks and a truck filled with U.S. troops began to fire at each other, believing they were confronting troops loyal to Noriega, whereas in reality both were north american units.

"I believe that they were carrying out a clean-up operation and shooting at anything that moved. They were trying to keep people from leaving their houses in order to carry out their work more easily," explained Maruja. Later they saw a helicopter which landed twice at the front steps of the Marriott Hotel—where Maruja and Juantxu were staying—in order to carry out U.S. dead and wounded resulting from clashes.

"The invasion was a Hollywood spectacular. I believe that the U.S. forces were experimenting with arms and playing war in Panama, apart from killing troops, some of whom I visited in the hospitals, although no one will ever know the real numbers.

"Those first days of the U.S. invasion were hysterical. I do not believe that Noriega was their first or even second objective, but rather, to have as few losses as possible so that U.S. citizens could eat their Christmas turkey according to their custom."[27]

15
The Pre-Planned Looting of Panama

Philip Wheaton

After the first days of the U.S. invasion, which involved bombing, killing, burning, media control and clean-up, a new phenomenon occurred just before Christmas: *massive looting*. Some photos and television reports partially revealed the fact that U.S. troops were "close by" the sacking activities but did nothing. Furthermore, almost nothing was said about this chaos by the U.S. military or government. The authors wondered at the time whether the looting might not have been planned by the U.S. psychological warfare team in order to provide Panamanians a kind of Christmas bonus, but we lacked hard evidence. The fact that the looting was pre-planned has now been confirmed.

In the first place, the U.S. troops were not "nearby" the looting, they were *right there!* First-hand reports and photos from both Panamanian and U.S. publications confirm their close proximity. Witnesses in Panama City and Colon told us that North American forces were all over the place; they were totally in control. In some cases they invited the looters in or indicated there would be no opposition. Furthermore, after it began, the U.S. troops could have stopped the looting at any time but did not. The obvious conclusion is that U.S. decision makers *allowed the looting to happen or encour-*

aged it. Why? Apparently, because the invasion, coming just before Christmas and following a year of terrible hardship, was seen by the invaders as providing a psychological outlet or escape valve for the tensions and anger created by the occupation. As a result, many of those looting felt that at least "they got something out of this mess."

In the second place, we have learned that the U.S. decision to allow or encourage the looting did not begin last July (1989) when General Thurman received his orders to prepare actively for the invasion, but *two years earlier!* The wife of an Episcopal priest in Colon told us that a computer trainer who worked for the U.S. Army (a civilian named Bob) and was privy to inside military information about the invasion planning told her about this detail as part of the overall strategy. The importance of this information is that it proves that frequently what happens in Third World countries and especially in Central America, especially during critical moments, is often not the result of indigenous or spontaneous events but of carefully executed decisions made in Washington, D.C.

While the looting projects a negative image on the Panamanian people, this event is really a mirror of how U.S. imperialism operates. Indeed, it is not dissimilar to the ancient practice of imperial armies sacking conquered nations.[28]

16
Why The U.S. Cover-up?
What Was Washington Hiding?

What was Washington afraid of? Why did the U.S. forces go to such lengths top cover up the results of an invasion which the Bush administration was publicly lauding and justifying to the U.S. Congress. There appear to be four reasons for such strange behavior by the U.S. military.

First, *to shift the sympathy of the N. American people away from the Panamanian victims to the 23 U.S. soldiers who died in the invasion.* Extensive coverage was given to those U.S. heros who died while almost no attention was paid to the suffering and dying of Panamanians. We remember, of course, how U.S. sympathy shifted during the Vietnam war to the Vietnamese people who were victims of our bombings and "search and destroy" missions (i.e., My Lai). So in Panama it appears that the strategy was to make the victims disappear (by not covering that part of the story nor allowing the facts to come out), thereby turning the aggressors into victims. As a result, Americans sat down to their Christmas meals with no guilt because the real victims of our aggression had not only disappeared ... *visually they never existed!*

Second, *because of rapid physical clean-up (of bodies and buildings), very few Panamanian families ever saw their loved ones dead or buried ... they simply disappeared.* Similarly, the investigatory efforts of Ramsey Clark three days after the invasion turned up very little: "It looked like a desert," he said. Most Panamanians therefore did not see much; they only heard the bombing and shooting. Furthermore, many first-hand witnesses were afraid to give their names; they were literally traumatized into silence. As a result, the victim nation was left with little to do but to grieve their losses.

Third, *by hiding the human and physical evidence of the invasion, the Pentagon covered up the human impact and suffering caused by its new and devastatingly destructive weapons.* In the above section—Panama: Testing Ground for New U.S. Weapons—Pentagon officials talked enthusiastically about how effective these weapons were and how they protected American lives but said nothing about the destructive impact these weapons had on the Panamanian people: bullets that explode internally, buildings that implode and stun, bombs that destroy and traumatize, flamethrowers that incinerate bodies, etc.

Fourth. by controlling the Panamanian media and maintaining propaganda influence over all crucial information, the United States conditions the victim population about what happened in the first place and towards passively accepting the invasion as necessary. The invasion was a singular success in the United States in large part because the U.S. media went along with the official government myths about the necessity for invading. The moral and political implications of this model of warfare are extremely troubling for they imply that whenever the United States decides to invade, Washington will determine who is to be eliminated (anyone who stands in its way), how to deceive both the victim and aggressor populations and who will serve in the new government and lead the military of the conquered country. This total war model is not only *grossly inhuman* in terms of the victim nation but *totally immoral* as a military strategy, completely contradicting the United States'own stated values.

Panamanian civilians killed in U.S. attack lying in a morgue in Panama City.

PANAMANIAN REALITIES AND U.S. MOTIVATIONS

17
"Worst Tragedy In Panamanian History"

Raul Leis

The author is one of the most knowledgeable and respected sociologists and political analysts in Panama.

"The U.S. military intervention of the Republic of Panama, its antecedents and consequences represent the worst tragedy ever suffered by the country in terms of human victims, material damage and moral impact in our entire republican history."

The economic damage caused by the invasion and looting fluctuates in value between $1.5 and $2 billion Balboas (the Balboa is on a par with the Dollar), with high levels of infrastructural damage and unemployment. According to the Chamber of Commerce, 10,000 employees will be left jobless and 5,000 more tenuous in terms of their labor rights. The effect of the invasion and looting upon public services—health centers, libraries, schools, museums, etc.—is incalculable. To this must be added the mass firing of public employees and the increasing instability for others since the new government came into office.

One has to remember what the state of the economy was at the time of the invasion due to the economic sanctions which had placed time of the invasion due to the economic sanctions which had placed upon Panama by the United States since 1988, especially fiscal and financial pressures. The Gross National Product had fallen about 25%. Fiscal income had dropped by 44% while investment programs and social services had declined by a similar amount. Capital flight from Panama is estimated at $24 billion, while exports had fallen by 11.3% and imports were down 35%. The construction industry had cut back by 60% causing the firing of 86% of the workers in that field. Commerce had declined by 28.3%. Unemployment was officially down 16% while the reality was closer to 25%. Those living at the level of 'critical poverty' ascended to between 33% and 40.2% of the total population over this two year period.

The North American sanctions included the freezing of $120 million in funds at the National Bank of Panama in the United States, the suspension of the fiscal obligations of 200 U.S. firms which had stopped paying their Panamanian taxes valued at $400 million annually, including money owed to the Panama Canal Commission. In addition, one has to add the suspension of Panama's sugar quota of 30,000 tons and the prohibition on U.S.loans, donations and economic assistance. Finally, the United States announced sanctions against Panama-flagging, those international merchant ships registered in Panama....

In synthesis, the framework of the invasion leads us to surmise that this is the worst cataclysm in the republican history of this nation, which is a country without earthquakes, hurricanes or other natural disasters. In a country which had a bloodless independence and has never been actively engaged in war ... the only major incidents before 1903 being the Spanish conquest some five centuries ago plus the War of a Thousand Days at the end of the past century, though we were then a part of Colombia. This invasion is also the worst of the twenty U.S. interventions into Panama by the United States, the first on April 15, 1856. Furthermore, this has been the most shameful invasion, since it was the first and only time a majority of the population approved of such a foreign aggression[29]

18
Drug Allegations Distort Noriega's Role

Esmeralda Brown

*Ms. Brown, the co-author, is a Panamanian citizen who
has lived in the USA for many years and works for the
Women's Division of the United Methodist Church to
the U.N. wrote this piece in early 1989.*

The allegations of drug trafficking by General Noriega have been
widely accepted in the United States, but is Noriega really the
problem in Panama and are drugs the real issue here? Let us examine
some facts: Panama is neither a producer nor a consumer of drugs.
The U.S. Drug Enforcement Agency (DEA) consistently singled
Panama out as a nation complying with U.S. requests for assistance in
this fight against drugs, as evidenced by many of the congratulatory
letters to Panamanian authorities, including General Noriega himself,
for their "excellent cooperation and effort with the U.S. government
agencies." A 1987 publication entitled '16 Years of Fighting Against
Drugs in Panama' contains countless DEA letters of commendation
to Panama.

It should also be noted that the indictments against General
Noriega were never taken seriously by Panamanians because they
were based on the word of three drug convicts who were promised
reduced jail sentences for testifying against him.

More importantly, the real issue is not Noriega or drugs but rather
the policy of the U.S. government towards Central America and the
Caribbean. U.S. strategy is either: a) to keep puppet governments in
power, as in El Salvador, Honduras, Grenada and Haiti, or, b) to put
back into power the old oligarchies that will guarantee the pro-tection
of U.S. geo-political interests, at the same time that they support U.S.
interventionist policies in the region (which are military, chauvinistic
and racist in nature).

At this point in time, the U.S. government has decided that
Panama must be castigated for opposing its interventionist policy, that
is, for creating the 'Contadora Group', a peace process which pressed
the Central American governments to resolve the regional conflicts

themselves through 'negotiated solutions' rather than by military solution as Washington wished.

Additionally, unlike other Central American countries, such as Honduras and El Salvador, which have facilitated U.S. use of their territories to deploy troops, allow contra camps and provide land and air support for incursions into Nicaragua, Panama has not allowed the use of its territory for such aggression against a sister republic.

Most Panamanians believe that the Reagan administration (and now Bush) created the present crisis in an attempt to renegotiate the Torrijos-Carter Treaties of 1977, thus guaranteeing U.S. presence in and influence over the Panama Canal, the Canal Zone and the military bases after the year 2,000. By creating an unstable situation within the country, the U.S. government can declare that there is a 'clear and present danger to the Panama Canal,' giving the United States the 'right' to intervene militarily to 'defend' the waterway.

It is clear that the present U.S. involvement in Panama's internal affairs (1989) is designed to facilitate the re-emergence of the oligarchy under the "civil Crusade" movement, which has the total support of the Reagan administration and who represent, in effect, the United States' 'new contras' against their own people by over-throwing the legitimate government of Panama.[30]

19
"The Noriega Case": U.S. Fear of Popular Uprising

Jose Eugenio Stoute

> *Mr. Stoute is an outstanding Panamanian political analyst who writes regularly for* Opinion Publica. *This is a letter directed to some relatives and friends who live in Argentina.*

I cannot give you my opinion (about Noriega) without first clarifying for you my literary analysis of this little tragic-comedy. I would say that it was that vacation which (Washington) tried to force on the little fraud (Noriega) which marked the point of no return in terms of the honeymoon between the U.S. government and the Noriega regime. Remember that *the fraud was between the two of them and had the blessing of the State Department.* The objective was to carry out a smooth transition from a dictatorship to a so-called democracy under the rationale that "nothing unusual is happening here." But Noriega's pranks pushed the well-planned strategy of the United States overboard, so that Washington suddenly realized that it would have to throw its ally in this complicity out of their band. However, that very isolation became dangerous for the United States' continued stable control of Panama.

Remember that it was in the Spring (1987) when the pressures to have Noriega take a vacation in Europe began. Then came the declaration of Diaz Herrera and the national insurrection by the Panamanian people (October 1988). That insurrection alerted the U.S. government to the danger *that the people might overthrow the dictatorship,* a force which the gringos had armed and pampered with such care. From that moment on, the White House realized that its only possibility for continued domination of the country was by cloaking its politics under the disguise of democracy and *preceding* the people in the task of overthrowing the dictatorship, so that in this way they could install in Panama a "true" democracy. This task was effectively fulfilled on Dec. 20th. Since then, the creators of this monster have presented themselves as those who liberated us from the monster. What a paradox!

Now you can more easily understand what you have called 'the Noriega case.' Can you imagine the Panamanian people listening on radio and television to this CIA agent—Manuel Antonio Noriega—confessing in court the secrets about his relationship with the U.S. government? Otherwise, he wouldn't have remained a puppet with his head on! This court process had to prevent any larger revelation (beyond the drugs), which is why they carried him to Miami. In this way, they convert the Panamanian judicial system into a mere extension of the U.S. judicial system. So say goodby to any hope for an independent judicial system here!

On the other hand, the crimes of which they accuse the dictator will go unpunished, because in the United States he will be judged for crimes different from those he committed in Panama against the Panamanian people. What an irony! As you can see, we are happy about our tragedy because we still keep on confusing the puppet with the puppeteer. But I don't think much time will pass before the people begin to awake from this nightmare and mystery story.[31]

20
Revealing Anecdotes On Robbery, Racism & Resistance

Philip Wheaton

During the month of February 1990, some revealing anecdotes were shared with me by Panamanians and that reflect some of the contradictions about this invasion and point to the difficulties facing those committed to building a new Panama.

The first involves a unique *robbery by the U.S. occupation forces*, reminiscent of World War II. The robbery included priceless treasures from the National Museum:

> In Buenos Aires, Argentina word came to the intellectual circles here that the North American forces had stolen the entire library of Dr. Ernesto Castillero Pimentel, along with the art collection of Noriega, valued in the millions of dollars, from the National Museum, thence taking it to the United States.... Incredible![32]

It is important to start with this imperial robbery because it represents not only a premeditated crime but more importantly the fact the gringos think they have the right to steal such treasures, precisely because they consider it a U.S. colony. This is similar to the sacking of conquered cities that empires have done down through the annals of history.

A second anecdote has to do with the *colonial aspect* of this invasion related to the looting which has already been discussed. This story comes from the Episcopal Church in Colon where the looting was criticized during a Sunday sermon to a group of middle-class West Indian Panamanian blacks. At that moment in the sermon, nearly every head in the congregation turned to his or her neighbor, their faces smiling sheepishly. The point is that for that traditional Episcopal congregation to have become involved in looting could only have happened because they felt it was O.K. to do it ... that the colonial leaders approved because certain military officials had given the signal it was all right to loot! This is a clear example of how colonial attitudes still influence some people's thinking in Panama.

Another aspect of the looting reported to me in Panama City reflects the *class nature* of the invasion. It involves the fact that in many cases when poor people—often dark-skinned persons—were running from the looting with stolen merchandise on their heads or backs through well-to-do neighborhoods, they were often stopped by white-skinned, well-off Panamanians carrying weapons who ordered the looters to turn over their TV sets and radios on threat of death. These goods were then confiscated personally and taken into the homes of these well-off residents. With the white, wealthy class now in power in Panama, the likelihood of such crude forms of exploiting the poor, as well as more sophisticated techniques, is very high.

My third anecdote involves the surprising *resistance* put up by the Panamanian Defense Forces and the Codepadis. Their motivation in resisting the Yankee invader was not the result of blind obedience to Noriega, as the U.S. press and Southern Command have continually claimed, but to genuine patriotism for which they were willing to sacrifice their lives.

Two *imperial responses* to this patriotic resistance should be highlighted: First, that U.S. troops did not want to engage these freedom fighters but tried in every way possible to annihilate them with high-powered weapons and bombs or overwhelm them with massive numbers. Reports have been received that some U.S. troops were even "afraid" of the Panamanians, or at least afraid of being killed. Second, that U.S. officials directing the invasion process went to great lengths to isolate these resistance fighters from the public, towards the end of stifling all such patriotic spirit and keeping it from the Panamanian people. The implications of these responses is obvious: Washington seeks a docile, colonized Panama, a people who silently accept the policies and slogans of the invader. But such a totally anti-democratic and anti-patriotic position only confirms the imperial nature of this invasion.[33]

21
Noriega or Bush: Which One Is More Shameless?

Interview with Chuchu Martínez

Introduction

Jesus "Chuchu" Martínez has never lost his spirit of adventure even at 61 years of age and after years of academic studies in Mexico, the USA, East Germany, Cuba, Chile and Spain. A student of Diego Rivera, Ortega y Gasset and Pablo Neruda, Chuchu is also a doctor of philosophy and one of the best poets in Panama. He also studied at the U.S. naval academy in Massachusetts and became an aviator and mathematician.

Impressed by the personality of General Omar Torrijos, Chuchu became in time one of Torrijos' closest confidant and a member of his "personal security" team. Chuchu knows almost every important person who has played a historic role in recent Central American history. After the assassination of Torrijos, Chuchu retired from the political scene in Panama though he remained a lieutenant in the Panamanian Defense Forces, until the invasion on Dec. 20th.

When did the United States begin planning the invasion?

[C.M.] The "gringos" were absolutely firm about not losing their military presence in Panama after the year 2,000. The problem was how to accomplish this goal. In the beginning, they counted on Noriega because they already had a close relationship with him. That failed. Still they went on counting on this man—Noriega—who is shameless, a drug trafficker and ambitious. To this shameless guy, they said: "Take your silver and go enjoy it in Paris." That's where they made their big mistake, because Noriega isn't a bandit as they thought; he doesn't sell himself for money, which he has now demonstrated. Noriega had lost everything and he knew perfectly well that they had this threat hanging over his head (the drug charge) which they offered to lift if he would leave power. But he refused.

The third attempt by the U.S. was to operate through a political opposition, but in the May 1989 elections again the gringos got stuck their foot into their mouth. Certainly there was fraud in the elections, but I don't know of any election ever in Panama that wasn't fraudulent. In this case, however, *the fraud came about via the gringos who gave the opposition lots of money just as they gave to the UNO opposition in Nicaragua.* But there was something more serious behind the White House position because Bush said: *"If Endara doesn't win, we invade."* This is Washington's so-called *democratic option*: either vote for Endara or we invade. So, the Panamanians went to the polls thinking that if Noriega's candidate wins, the Yankees will either kill Noriega or invade. . . .

But the troubling thing is that the people welcomed the gringos.

We Panamanians have been going through a goddamn economic crisis for years and the Noriega government didn't distinguish itself by taking any popular measures to counter those sanctions. To the contrary, the laws of war he enacted were contrary to the interests of the people. There is only one progressive thing about Noriega's government: his clash with the Empire . . . but there was no national program to go with it to satisfy their needs. On the other hand, the people faced the North Americans and paid for it with 3,000 lives. The volume of U.S. firepower and the refinement of their weapons is incredible. They did in Panama more or less what Hitler did in Spain, using it as a practice ground for the weapons he would use during World War II. Here in Panama, the gringos used their newest weapons: helicopters, that plane that flies around in circles like a goddamn electronic laboratory, practicing their galaxy war here.

Did you ever try to convince Noriega to change?

No, I never spoke with him. I worked very closely with Torrijos but never with Noriega. A series of coincidences showed me how God was protecting me even though I'm an atheist. I worked very closely with Col. Diaz (Herrera) when he rose up against Noriega and made his declarations to the press. Well, Col. Diaz is crazy but God protected me. At a given moment, Diaz ordered me arrested and told me that he was going to put me in a hole (a grave). But it appears that Noriega intervened and must have reasoned: "If Col. Diaz is against

Chuchu, Chuchu must be with me." So, instead of punishing me, the military close to Col. Diaz advanced me in rank from second to first lieutenant. But I never talked with Noriega.

What lesson can the popular movements in Latin America draw from this intervention?

One is that Bush is trying to say to Latin America: "you see what will happen to you if you don't do what I want." The other lesson that Bush is giving to the North American public involves saying: "you see what I am capable of, you who go around saying I'm a coward and weak-hearted." It's the attitude of a pimp who has to prove his manhood.

But the Panamanians also proved something by their resistance, which is evident by the number of deaths we suffered, something without precedent in Latin America. Remember, those people didn't die of malaria. Another lesson is the dirty one left by some sectors of the middle class—more than the oligarchy which was naturally defending its economic interests—but the middle class went around kissing North Americans and waving their little flags. So Latin America can learn from their dirty behavior because such sectors are to be found throughout the hemisphere.

Perhaps the most important lesson that the gringos gave those of us who want to do something about this involves what they used to say during the Middle Ages: *Extra ecclesium nula salus*, "outside the Church you can do nothing." Today, however, the church has a commitment to the people. Torrijos knew this lesson and at one time said—though he didn't do it—"You can't have a national identity sufficiently strong to oppose an aggression of this magnitude if you haven't identified with the people; if the people aren't behind you." But the people weren't behind Torrijos.[34]

Notes

24. *Pensamiento Propio*, Feb. 1990, op. cit., p. 28.
25. Ibid., p. 29.
26. Cecilio ER. Simon E., Testimony, CODEHUCA, Document # 13, Panama, Jan. 13, 1990.

27. *Liberacion, MLN-29-XI, Panama, Feb., 1990, Maruja Torres, "Panama era una locura,"* p. 4.
28. Philip Wheaton interview with Helen Waldron in Colon, Feb. 17, 1990.
29. CEASPA, *Este Pais, Mes a Mes,* Panama, Feb. 1990, No. 26, Raul Leis, "Diez Ideas Sobre El Panama De Hoy," pp. 13-14.
30. Esmeralda Brown, "The Changing World Order-Third World Prospectives: *Current Situation in Panama,"* American Friends Service Committee, Boston, Mass., Women's Workshop, Mar. 21,1989, pp. 2-4.
31. *Opinion Publica,* Feb. 1990, op. cit., Jose Eugenio Stoute, "El caso Noriega," p. 16.
32. Jose E. Stoute, "El caso Noriega," *Opinion Publica,* Feb. 1990, op. cit., p. 16.
33. Philip Wheaton, interviews with a Panamanian writer and a Chilean woman from a upper middle-class neighborhood, and with West Indians in Margarita, Colón, February 14-19, 1990.
34. *Pensamiento Propio,* Jan/Feb., 1990, op. cit., pp. 34-35.

U.S. soldiers shared kisses and sweets with Panamanians as part of their daily chores. Here two soldiers are holding the party flag of the Christian Democratic Party which Washington supported.

PART II

HOW PANAMANIAN SOVEREIGNTY CHALLENGED U.S. IMPERIALISM: THE FOUR CRUCIAL ISSUES THAT LED TO THE INVASION

INTRODUCTION: FOUR CRUCIAL ISSUES
LEADING TO THE INVASION

Xabier Gorostiaga

The military intervention and U.S. occupation of Panama and
the creation of an artificial and puppet government on a
military base within the Canal Zone are the best historical
evidence that the new international dynamics have no validity
in Central America.[1]

These words by Xabier Gorostiaga, a Jesuit priest and nationalized
Panamanian citizen, followed from his view that though the Berlin
wall has been dismantled in Europe, the United States maintains its
dominant satellite in Central America and the Caribbean. As an
advisor to General Torrijos between 1971 and 1975, during the
development of the Canal treaties, Gorostiaga states bluntly that "the
Cold War is not over in Central America." Indeed, he goes so far as
to say that "unless the international community assists Panama in
finding a political solution to this crisis, the whole region will continue
to be a zone of conflict during the 1990s."

Gorostiaga then proceeded to outline what he considers to be the
four crucial issues or focuses (*ejes*) which led to the U.S. invasion of
Panama on December 20, 1989:

We cannot understand the Panamanian crisis in terms of the

figure of General Noriega. The crisis has *four fundamental focuses:*

a) the treaties and the recent phase of implementation;
b) the systematic dismantling of the ethos of Torrijos (*torrijismo*);
c) the recreation of the oligarchy and other rightist forces; and,
d) the elimination of the role of Japan in its attempt to control Panama as its exclusive financial zone.[2]

The uniqueness of these four crucial issues is that none of these points were highlighted by the White House which concentrated on the person and deeds of Manuel Noriega. When Dr. Gorostiaga was asked what role Noriega did play in precipitating the intervention, he replied:

> We the peoples of Central America, have an important lesson to learn: national sovereignty must be linked to popular sovereignty. Putting national sovereignty in the hands of corrupt figures like Noriega produces no good. Noriega was incapable of offering any resistance to the USA and abandoned the people to the invading forces, leaving them—often the very poor—to defend their nation in an anarchical fashion. During the preceding year and a half, the people sabotaged an economy which denied them basic survival. This situation led to tremendous internal confusion in Panama. I would imagine that the Panamanian people are cursing both the U.S. invasion and Noriega. Disenchantment and disillusionment have produced passivity. But the United States should be careful not to misjudge this loss of nationalism which the Panamanian people have never lost, for it could be reborn, even though at this moment it is dormant because of a profoundly complex crisis.[3]

The complexity of the Panamanian crisis is not only the product of a long history but of a dialectic struggle between *the Panamanian people in search of sovereignty while living under the imperial eagle.* Whereas Washington would have us believe that the invasion was a simple event related to the removal of one evil leader or the United States' concern for democracy, in fact, its fundamental motivation was U.S. military control over Panama after the year 2,000. The time-table for Panama to achieve complete sovereignty was reaching a critical moment, with the United States facing the danger of losing its century-long control over the Isthmus. That is what led to the invasion. As Gorostiaga notes,

> neither U.S. defense of the canal nor judicial prosecution of Noriega justified an invasion which cost possibly a thousand lives or more, tremendous suffering and damage to the country, an action that has not resolved but complicated the emergence of democracy in Panama now under a colonial government.[4]

The following section is an historical study of these four issues in light of Panama's struggle for sovereignty. Down through the years, Washington has used as its excuse for remaining in the Zone "the threat to the Canal," a threat never carried out by anyone until the United States itself closed down the Canal (briefly) in 1989! Many such half-truths cloak the real motivations behind this invasion, including the fact that a majority of the invading forces were Spanish-speaking troops: Puerto Ricans, Dominicans and Chicanos, indeed, the first "gringo" to die was a Peruvian. As Don Quixote once said to Sancho: "This doesn't smell like amber to me." Out task here is to find the amber; to tell the truth.

Omar Torrijos understood the conflict involved with a relationship with the U.S. In the face of U.S. superiority, Torrijos developed a foreign policy of alliances which prevented Washington from isolating Panama and its national objectives.

THE CARTER-TORRIJOS TREATIES: A THREAT TO U.S. REGIONAL CONTROL

1
Creating the Republic Under the American Eagle

Dr. Ernesto Castillero Pimentel[5]

The first official act between the U.S. government and the Republic of Panama was marked by deception and betrayal, foreshadowing a future of unjust agreements and Panamanian capitulations. Because the Senate of the Republic of Panama refused to ratify the Herran-Hay Treaty, which would have deeded the Canal Zone to the United States within the Department of Panama belonging to Colombia, the State Department together with the director of the French Canal Company, Phillippe Bunau-Varilla, were forced to employ the only alternative left to them: create a Republic out of the Panamanian Isthmus and then require that Republic to turn over its jurisdictional rights in the Zone to the United States.

Bunau-Varilla's interest was tied to the bankruptcy of his Canal Company and finding a way to sell the rights to the Company to the U.S. government, harking back to the failed French effort to build a Canal across the Isthmus between 1879 and 1888. This led him to collaborate with the U.S. expansionists by serving as a mediator between Washington and those conspiring against Colombia for independence in the Isthmus. In the case of both the Frenchman and the Gringos, the issue of *Panamanian sovereignty and its rights were incidental.* The power which implemented this imperial strategy arrived off the coast of Panama in 1903 in the form of eleven U.S. battleships and destroyers from which Mariners landed forcing the Colombian troops to retreat from Colon.

Next, Bunau-Varilla—from his room in the Waldorf Astoria Hotel in New York City—asked the Panamanian leaders to name him Special Envoy to the United States for the new Republic, as yet unrecognized by any nation in the world. On Nov. 6, 1903, he received the following telegram:

> The Junta of the Provisional Government names you Special Envoy and Minister Plenipotentiary before the Government of the United States, with full powers to work out negotiations of a political and financial nature.
> —Signed, J. A. ARANGO, FREDERICO BOYD, TOMAS ARIAS.[6]

But while Bunau-Varilla was given power to negotiate, he was not authorized to sign any treaty. On that same day, the United States extended *de facto* recognition to the Government of the Republic of Panama. The following day, Bunau-Varilla notified the U.S. Secretary of State, John Hay, of his authorization and together the two men began to negotiate the conditions of the treaty. The Frenchman knew full well that at that very moment a Panamanian Commission was leaving Panama by ship to come to the United States to ratify and sign the treaty. However, fearing the Commission might place conditions on the treaty that were unacceptable to the U.S. Senate, Bunau-Varilla decided "to broadly extend the portion of sovereignty granted to the United States in the (rejected) Herran-Hay Treaty" and to sign the document as quickly as possible. Therefore, Bunau-Varilla gave John Hay a *concession on sovereignty en bloc,* a formula which would grant the United States

> all rights, powers and authority which the United States will exercise and possess *as if sovereign over the territory;* completely excluding the exercise of those sovereign rights, powers and authority granted only by the Republic of Panama.[7]

With this *carte blanche* condition, the U.S. Senate approved the arrangement on Nov.18, 1903 and the Hay-Bunau-Varilla Treaty was signed into law, *without a single Panamanian being present!* At that very moment, the Panamanian delegation was travelling by train from New York to Washington, unaware of what was transpiring. When they arrived in Washington, they were greeted by Bunau-Varilla with the words: "The Republic of Panama from this day on is under the protection of the United States. I have just signed the Canal Treaty."[8]

Perhaps the most revealing statement made by this conniving Frenchman reflects not only the imperial nature of the 1903 agreement but that of the invasion of Panama in 1989, eighty-six years later:

By extending protective wings over the territory of "our" Republic, the American Eagle has sanctified it and rescued it from the unnecessary and ruinous barbarisms of civil war, in order to consecrate it to that destiny to which Providence has assigned it: the service of Humanity and the progress of Civilization.[9]

It was this same American Eagle which swooped down from the skies on December 20 to bomb and kill Panamanians in order to save it from civil strife, and it is today under the Eagle of U.S. imperialism that the new struggle for Panamanian sovereign must begin.

2
U.S. Non-Compliance On Its WWII Military Bases Agreement

Gregorio Selser[10]

Following the Japanese attack on Pearl Harbor on December 7, 1941, Panama Declared war on Japan on December 8, as did the other Caribbean basin countries then dominated by U.S. policy: Nicaragua, Cuba, Guatemala, the Dominican Republic and Haiti. On May 18, 1942, President Franklin D. Roosevelt entered into an agreement with the Republic of Panama for the rental of 134 defense posts (*Sitios de Defensa*), comprising 37,000 acres of land. In addition to only paying minimal rent, the United States promised to return all of these posts and their lands to Panama one month after the cessation of World War II hostilities.

On Sept. 1, 1946, when the Panamanian government expressly requested "the return and turning over of all the defense posts which the United States is still using in light of Panama's sovereignty and rights"[11], president Harry Truman pretended he didn't know about the promise made by his predecessor. The State Department stalled and then agreed to withdraw from 51 posts while still holding on to 83 others. When the Government of Panama, through its National Assembly, demanded full compliance with the agreement, General Crittenberger said the United States would withdraw from another 27 sites while intending to hold on to the Rio Hato air base and other locations. Upon further pressure from the Assembly, Washington responded that there was a "difference of opinion" about the promise made by James Byrnes in 1945 to withdraw. This created increasing resentment on the part of the Panamanian people, indeed, an emotional *"climate of agitation and hatred against the United States."*[12]

Next, a National Commission was created to approach General Hines, then U.S. ambassador to Panama, directing him to take this matter directly to president Truman. The White House responded by emphasizing "the fulfillment of *our joint responsibilities* for the adequate protection of the Canal"—code language for continuing U.S. control. While Washington did return 20 more sites, it held on to Rio Hato and 35 others, proposing a twenty year rental for Rio Hato and a five year contract for 12 radar installations. On Dec. 10, 1946, a Filos-Hines "executive accord" was signed (so the matter wouldn't have to go to the Senate for ratification) in which the United States offered to rent 13 bases comprising 28,838 acres of land for approximately $28,000 annually, or about $1 per acre!

When the National Assembly received the details of the accord on December 12, hundreds of Panamanian students from the National Institute protested, with the result that many students were wounded by police repression, one seriously. That student, Sebastian Tapia, became "the flag of opposition", a cause taken up by various student organizations who rejected the Filos-Hines accord. Notwithstanding opposition to these protests from Panama's agro-industrial elite (oligarchy) who saw in this rejection possible financial loss for the economy, which had been greatly stimulated by World War II, the accord was not accepted. The mounting agitation arose not from the rental of the bases *per se* but the fact that "the United States had not complied with its solemn promise made in the 1942 agreement."[13]

With that rejection, resentment calmed down. Panama had won its first open challenge of U.S. domination even though the remaining sites were not returned. The issue dragged on for several years until 1952 when General Dwight Eisenhower became president. That same year, José Antonio Remón became president of Panama, through a fraudulent election financed by the United States. Even though Remon's electoral slogan related to the defense posts said, "Neither millions nor crumbs: we want justice," his election and presidency represented a coalition of support from the oligarchy, military and United States. In order to reach an accord, Washington agreed to upgrade the National Police into a National Guard, presumably symbolizing greater Panamanian independence, although the State Department no doubt saw this as yet another instrument of its own; a praetorian guard.

When the Remón-Eisenhower Treaty for Mutual Understanding and Cooperation was finally signed in 1953, it produced a deepening political polarization in Panama. On the one hand, "the oligarchic strategy of claims upon the North Americans was always motivated by economics never by principle,"[14] while internally there was always the threat of reprisal, as happened when president Remon was assassinated in 1955. On the other hand, the Treaty sowed the seeds in the students which gradually developed into a nationalistic spirit, something rare or sporadic up to that time in Panama. Furthermore, unlike the case of Nicaragua, the Panamanian National Guard was not linked to a dictator. Rather, it was organized during this period of rising nationalism, which contributed to the Guard's sense of patriotism. As a result, in 1960 the National Assembly declared that "the flag of Panama should fly over *our territory* in the Canal Zone."[15] This became the battle cry during the next stage in this dialectic process between U.S. arrogance and Panamanian sovereignty.

3
Panama Explodes: The 1964 Flag Riots

Aristides Martinez Ortega[16]

The immediate cause of the "flag riots" of January 9, 1964 was the non-compliance by U.S. citizens in the Canal Zone with the orders of the U.S. military commander. Towards the end of December 1963, General Fleming began to implement the flag agreement signed by the governments of Panama and the United States which recognized the Canal Zone to be *de jure* Panamanian territory, which meant that the Panamanian flag was to be flown together with the American flag wherever Zone officials had previously established flag sites.

To reduce the number of Panamanian flags which might eventually have to be raised in the Zone, U.S. authorities unilaterally and in violation of the spirit of the agreement, dismantled a number of flag installations in the Zone, among others those in front of the Governor's residence and at the Port Captain's Building in Balboa. In line with this tactic, during the first days of 1964, General Fleming issued orders for the dismantling of flag poles in front of the public schools in the Zone.

U.S. students at eight of the public schools in the Zone, including Balboa High School, acted to block this order. To prevent the authorities from lowering the American flag, the students began to mount around-the-clock vigils in front of their schools, urged on by their parents and with the tacit approval of the Zone police. On January 7 and 8, students and parents demonstrated outside the Governor's residence, demanding that General Fleming raise the American flag there in contempt of the agreement with Panama. The Panamanian press gave extensive coverage to the American protest, provoking a wave of indignation among Panamanian students. The anger was not so much against the actions of the American civilians in the Zone as against the complicity of Zone authorities with the demonstrations, since it implied an official refusal to recognize the terms of the agreement.

The initial violence began on January 9 when American students decided to keep any Panamanian flag out of what they considered to be "their" territory. At the end of classes that day in Panama City,

Panamanian students at the Instituto Nacional (high school) located near the boundary between the City and the Zone, petitioned their principal to turn over the school's national flag in order to carry it into the Zone and raise it on the flag pole at Balboa High School. A delegation of these students had gone to the Balboa H.S. the day before informing authorities of their intention. The action was intended to be a peaceful symbolic affirmation of Panama's rights in the Zone, affirmed by the 1963 agreement signed by president John F. Kennedy.

When some 200 Panamanian students entered the Zone, they were stopped by a cordon of police set up to deny them access, but after protracted negotiations, it was agreed that a delegation of six students could walk to the Balboa school under protection from the Zonian police, would raise the Panamanian flag and sing the national anthem. They carried a banner which read: "Panama is sovereign in the Canal Zone." When they arrived at the high school, a large, angry crowd of U.S. Zonian students and their parents had gathered in front of the school. As the delegation approached, they were greeted by jeers and taunts from the crowd. When they attempted to sing the Panamanian national anthem, they were shoved about and hit by mobs of U.S. students encouraged by their parents. Instead of protecting the delegation, the Zone police joined in the provocation. One of the police ripped the flag from the Panamanian students.

The delegation was forced to retreat towards the "border" where their fellow students were waiting, unable to assist their friends because of the cordon of police wielding clubs. Harassed verbally and physically, pursued by police and patrol cars, the students withdrew into Panama City, taking their torn flag with them. By 6:30 P.M. the news of the incident had spread across Panama City, inspiring small groups of unarmed young people to move spontaneously into the Zone carrying Panamanian flags. They were met by gunfire from the Zone police and Zonian civilians armed with shotguns, producing the first serious casualties. Around 8 P.M., General O'Meare assumed military command over the Zone in the absence of General Fleming and shortly thereafter, U.S. Army units equipped for combat and supported by tanks began to take up positions along the Zone boundary. Once again, small bands of Panamanians attempted to enter the Zone with flags in defiance of this new threat, but they were thrown back by machine gun and rifle fire from the American soldiers. The fusillade continued throughout the night and into the early morning hours of January 10.

During the night of Jan. 9, demonstrations also developed in Colón, where units of the National Guard tried unsuccessfully to hold back demonstrators. Many were able to reach the Zone. There, as in Panama City, the protestors were met not with tear gas or fire hoses but with automatic and rifle fire, causing 3 deaths and 141 wounded. By the end of the riots, a total of 21 Panamanians had been killed and over 400 wounded, leading to a massive funeral procession through the streets of Panama City, with the country's leaders accompanying thousands of students and workers. On January 10, 1964, Panama broke diplomatic relations with the United States. Foreign Minister Galileo Solis petitioned the OAS while Aquilino Boyd, Panama's ambassador to the United Nations, declared:

> In view of the long history of U.S. provocations against Panama, which exploded into open violence yesterday, we Panamanians will hold as heros and martyrs each and every one of our compatriots who have lost their lives in the aggression which continues unabated as I speak.
>
> The present status of the Canal Zone, which is and will be a source of daily and permanent discord, must be altered. Panama cannot remain subject to unfair treaties imposed against its legitimate rights and injurious to its very existence as a nation.... [17]

4
Talk, Torrijos and the Treaties: The Gradual Emergence of a National Consciousness

Gregorio Selser[18]

> *This brief examination of the role of Omar Torrijos and the process leading to the 1977 Treaties is not intended to be a complete history of that slow, complex process but merely a synthesis of the gradual emergence of a national consciousness of Panama's sovereign rights*

Following the January 9th conflict, Panama was politically boiling, and popular protests continued unabated. The patriotism of the students had pulled Panama out of decades of paralysis and apathy. Notwithstanding the moderate language used by president Roberto Chiari, especially in light of his well-known sympathies for the United States, it was clear that something very deep had occurred inside the Panamanian psyche, changing the conventional relations between the two countries. The Panamanian flag, as a symbol of its sovereignty, took on a special dimension in the process of this "conscientization."

This new determination, plus the deaths of the twenty-one Panamanians coupled with the breaking of diplomatic relations, forced president Lyndon Johnson to take Panama and the question of the "unjust treaty of 1903" seriously. On January 10, he called president Chiari to announce he was sending Thomas Mann to "re-establish peace" and open discussions on the renegotiation of the 1903 Treaty, saying:

> We are fully conscious that the demands which the Government of Panama and the majority of the Panamanian people are making do not arise from any malice or hatred towards the United States. They are based on a deep sense of the sincerity and just needs which Panama has.... We are prepared to examine all these differences which now divide us and all the problems which the Government of Panama may wish to bring before us.... [19]

By April 3rd, Panama and the United States had reestablished diplomatic relations as part of the mandate of an OAS Peace Commission to get at the causes of the conflict and take the first steps towards "a just and fair agreement" between the two countries. But the flag riots had also produced important internal changes in Panama. On May 10, 1964, Marco Robles was elected president of Panama over the traditional populist Arnulfo Arias Madrid, because the National Guard had vetoed Arias' candidacy. That veto reflected an alliance between the United States, the military and the traditional oligarchy, which Robles represented. As historian Ernesto Castillero reflects:

> Power continued in the hands of the traditional oligarchic sectors, organized in parties and mini-parties in defense of

personal and vested economic interests, based on a wave of
fear about international communism, sustained by the traditional domestic government which was a puppet to "Uncle
Sam"....[20]

Over the next four years, the process of moving towards a new
treaty was extremely slow and characterized principally by talk. On
Sept. 25, 1965, a Joint Declaration Robles-Johnson was published
stating that "the primary objective of the new treaty will be to provide
an appropriate political, economic and social integration of the
territory used for the operation of the Canal (Zone) with the rest of
the Republic of Panama." On June 22, 1967, a U.S.-Panamanian
Commission announced the existence of three projects as guidelines
for a new treaty, later known as the "Three-in-One Treaty". It called
for granting concessions to the United States for building a sea-level
Canal, eliminating the "neutrality" concept of the Canal and calling
for the legalization of the U.S. bases in the Zone. However, instead
of attacking the fundamental issue of dependency and sovereignty, the
3-in-1 Treaty focused on new elements within the old relationship.

Feelings about this treaty ran so deep and the issues it raised were
potentially so explosive that the whole Canal issue was tabled for the
1968 electoral campaign. The election was won by Arnulfo Arias who
defeated Robles on the basis of buying his political clientele and of
personality mudslinging in "one of the most violent, dirtiest, shameful
and rude campaigns ever seen in the history of our Republic ... and
carried out in a climate of extreme tension and anguish."[21] The
combination of a treaty process which was going nowhere, a dirty
democratic election and the traditional hostilities between the National Guard and Arnulfo Arias provided the context for the military coup
of 1968, in which General Omar Torrijos and others removed Arias
from power and moved towards establishing a new model of government.

Revealing his politics of intuition, Torrijos later gave an interview
to a newspaper in which he reflected back on that crucial step taken
in 1968:

From the moment I and my *companeros* in arms assumed
power, we decided not to form a military government but gave

ourselves to the task of incorporating into it, with their agreement of course, the best young leaders of the progressive left, along with values that could be rescued from the moderate right. From that equation which, had as its object to add not subtract, to build not destroy, and to work full time and not by the clock, towards ending injustice, for the dignity of the Panamanian people and to exalt without vacillating the one religion which unites us all: the struggle to recover the sovereignty and promote an integrated development of the country.[22]

Space doesn't allow us to discuss the attempted coup against Torrijos in 1969, except to say that the majority of the National Guard officers remained loyal to him and that Lt. Col. Manuel Antonio Noriega, in the city of David, played a key role in helping Torrijos return to the country and to power, as a result of which Noriega became head of military intelligence, G-2.

One of Torrijos' two primary goals for his government was the recovery of the Canal and Canal Zone for Panama. In 1967, Panama's foreign minister Juan Antonio Tack, rejected the 3-in-1 treaty as unsatisfactory as a means of eliminating the conflict between the two countries. With Torrijos in power, Tack's legal and moral objections to that treaty took on political power, forcing president Richard Nixon in 1970 to deal with this problem. Nixon's position was that any such treaty must have an indefinite time-limit as a pre-condition, a position rejected by Torrijos, who in 1971 said to the people:

Omar Torrijos is going to accompany you and the 6,000 guns of the National Guard will be there to defend the integrity and dignity of this people. Because when a people begin the process of decolonization, two things can happen: either they completely colonize us or they have to take the whole canopy of colonialism away. And they're going to take it away, gentlemen; they're going to take it away.[23]

Torrijos' language as well as his personal philosophy was direct and without finesse. He never liked to read speeches but preferred to improvise. He didn't mind making mistakes as long as the point was clear. In this spirit, Torrijos decided to raise the ante for the United States by taking the Canal issue to the United Nations, so that the whole world could know what was going on in Panama. Specifically, this diplomatic offensive had as its objective to create an international consciousness by taking their national problem to a world forum. Though it is true that Panama got strong support from the socialist bloc, mainly Cuba and the Soviet Union, Panama's position was not leftist but non-aligned. As Torrijos said before the United Nations: "Panama doesn't go outside with an umbrella when it rains in Moscow. That's a lie. Nor do we put on an overcoat when it's snowing in Washington. That's a lie. Panama is seeking it's own solution . . . . "[24]

The strategy was successful. By 1973, the United States stood almost alone on the issue of Panama's right to control the Canal Zone. Furthermore, a division developed between the State Department and the Pentagon, foreshadowing a similar tension which arose again in recent years, especially between 1986 and 1988. In that earlier preriod, Jack Hood Vaughn, Under-Secretary of State for Inter-American Affairs, challenged the Pentagon's position:

> Panama has risen up to test the supremacy of the Pentagon in determining our foreign policy. Will the United States continue to allow its military planners, with their obvious insensibility towards the force of nationalistic movements (referring then to Vietnam), to be the ones who make the decisions?[25]

But Vaughn's voice was the exception. Others, like that of John Scali, U.S. representative to the United Nations, argued that Panama had received great financial benefit from the relationship. But Tack challenged this argument, emphasizing how much more the United States had benefited from the arrangement. More pointedly, Tack asked why, after nine years of discussions, negotiations towards a new treaty had not advanced. Because, he said, the United States intends to maintain its military position in the Isthmus in perpetuity. In a unique decision, the United Nations voted to hold a special session on this issue held in Panama during March 1973. This session produced a resolution favorable to Panama which the United States vetoed. Torrijos responded angrily to that veto:

That veto, that projectile fired from Panama offended the feelings of all free men in the world.... It was not launched against a small country, because this nation is essentially a mystical matter, and against the mystical no effective projectile has yet been invented. Rather, this was a veto of arrogance, a projectile of arrogance, by a great power which says to the little countries that the U.S. is not going to allow anyone to keep fighting for their freedom.[26]

While that veto led to an immediate impasse in the negotiations, it served as the context for the Carter administration to decide in 1976-77 that it was time to open the Canal question to genuine dialogue and the drawing up of a new treaty. Thus the Carter-Torrijos Treaties of 1977 represented *a U.S. response to Panama's popular and military demands for sovereignty,* not—as portrayed by the Carter administration—the result merely of a liberal Democratic initiative.

However, the Treaties contained some serious loopholes, reinforced by last minute amendments which left open the possibility of U.S. intervention *if there was either an external threat or an internal instability* in Panama. While these conditions somewhat satisfied the conservatives in the Senate, the Treaties were hotly debated and only approved by a one-vote margin. From the Panamanian side, these loopholes led Torrijos to admit that Panama would be living

under the umbrella of the Pentagon (for the) ... twenty-three years during which these military bases will remain in our country, converting Panama into a strategic objective of reprisal and because we are signing a neutrality treaty which places us under the defensive umbrella of the Pentagon, a pact which future generations, if they don't administer it carefully could become an instrument for permanent intervention.[27]

Notes

1. *Barricada*, Dec. 22, 1989, Interview with Xabier Gorostiaga, "La invasion, el Canal y la guerra fria," Managua, p. 3.
2. Ibid.
3. *Pensamiento Propio*, Jan/Feb 1990, op. cit., p. 1.

4. Ibid.
5. EPICA, *Panama: Sovereignty For A Land Divided*, Washington, D.C., 1976, "Strange Circumstances Under Which the United States Acquired the Panama Canal Zone" by Dr.Ernesto Castillero Pimentel, pp. 19-23.
6. Bunau-Varilla, Phillippe, *Panama: The Creation, Destruction and Resurrection*, New York, 1920, p. 349.
7. Ibid., pp. 368-369.
8. p. 378.
9. p. 352.
10. Gregorio Selser, *Panama: Erase Un Pais A Un Canal Pegado*, "La Lucha Por Modificar El Tratado Inicuo," Mexico, D.F., Universidad Obrera de Mexico, 1989, p. 49ff.
11. Ibid., p. 59.
12. Jules Dubois, *Danger Over Panama*, New York, Bobbs-Merrill, 1964, p. 170.
13. Ricardo J. Alfaro, "Las bases, la opinion norteamericana y la verdad," Panama-Dominical, Panama, Jan. 4, 1948.
14. Humberto E. Ricord, *Relaciones entre Panama y Estado Unidos*, Panama, Biblioteca Nuevo, Panama, 1973.
15. Gregorio Selser, *Panama Erase...*, op. cit., p. 81.
16. EPICA, *Panama: Sovereignty For A Land Divided*, op. cit., taken from *Loteria*, Panama, October 1971, pp. 177-186.
17. Jacinto Rivera, Jr., "Significado Profundo del 9 de enero de 1964," *Relaciones Entre Panama y los Estados Unidos*, Ministerio de Educacion, Panama, 1974, translated by John Beverly. See also *Loteria*, No. 191. Panama, October, 1977, pp. 187-188.
18. Gregorio Selser, *Panama: Erase...*, op. cit., Chaps III and IV, pp. 85-187, summarized.
19. Ibid., p. 98.
20. Carlos Manuel Gastiazoro, et al, *La historia de Panama en sus textos*, EUPAN, Panama, 1980, pp. 321-323.
21. Ibid., p. 323.
22. Michel Labrut, *Este es Omar Torrijos*, Litografia Enan, Panama, 1982.
23. Ibid., p. 122.
24. Omar Torrijos Herrera, *Nuestra Revolucion*, Republica de Panama, Ministerio de Relaciones Exteriores, Departamento de Informacion, Panama, Dec. 1974, pp. 131-134.
25. E. Bradford Burns, "Panama's Struggle for its Independence," *Current History*, New York, Jan 1974, p. 19; See also, *Miami Herald*, March 14, 1973.
26. Omar Torrijos, talk given at close of the Campana de Alfabetizacion de la FEP, March 25, 1973, Panama.
27. Gregorio Selser, *Panama: Erase...*, op. cit., p. 179.

DISMANTLING TORRIJOS' MILITARY POPULISM: TEARING DOWN "OPERATION SOVEREIGNTY"

5
Omar Torrijos' Popularity, Vision & Assassination

Taken from interviews with José de Jesús Martínez[28]
confidant of General Omar Torrijos

To understand the U.S. invasion of Panama in 1989, one must appreciate the contradictory perspectives that existed around the 1977 Canal Treaties: in Washington, deep divisions among the American public about the wisdom of such an action versus Panamanian enthusiasm making General Omar Torrijos a hero. Whereas Torrijos incarnated Panama's nationalistic sense of pride, Jimmy Carter was hated by the Republican party and at least half of the American public who felt we had "given away" the Canal. From the moment of the Treaty signing, reactionary forces in the United States began planning how to undo the intention of the Treaties despite their legality. Such a reversal of public opinion would be a far more difficult task in the case of Panama since in its plebiscite, the Panamanian people voted 66% to 33% in favor of the Treaties.

The anti-treaty Republican forces were clear that Omar Torrijos was their foremost obstacle. Torrijos, reflecting scepticism about the

Treaties, which he reluctantly signed and were ratified into law in 1979, refused to attend the Panamanian celebration of the Treaties. He did he not believe that the Treaties would guarantee Panama's recovery of the Zone

> ending perpetuity (as a treaty condition) ... implies more than a juridical victory, (our goal) is the end of the real and physical occupation of our territory. I don't want to go down in history; I want to enter the Zone.[29]

Torrijos knew there were powerful forces intent on seeing that Panama never been given full sovereignty, i.e., control over the Canal. On the one hand, Ronald Reagan, the man who defeated Carter in the 1980 election, had been the primary opponent of the Canal Treaties, using the following slogan to justify his opposition to it: *"We bought it, we paid for it, we built it, it is ours and it should continue to be ours."* Other key persons opposing the Treaties were the three signers of the *Santa Fe Document*—a document which totally opposed the Treaties—General Gordon Sumner, Prof. Lewis Tambs and Roger Fontaine. All three men were given key Latin American posts in the new Reagan administration.

So instead of celebrating a victory in 1979, the Panamanian people might well have been more mindful of Torrijos' warning about the "Fifth Frontier" in Panama. This term refers to the fact that whereas Panama has four other frontiers—the Caribbean to the north, the Pacific Ocean to the south, Colombia to its east and Costa Rica to its west—there was a *fifth frontier* "in the very center of the very heart of the Isthmus". The Southern Command, that military complex which dominates all life in the Zone, is a presence that casts a dark shadow over Panama's supposed victory.

Omar Torrijos Herrera was known to Chuchu Martinez and many of his intimates as "My General", a term of affection, symbolizing not an oppressive dictatorship but a progressive strongman who became the primary advocate of sovereignty for Panama. Moreover, he was very popular among the poor and working class communities, not surprising since he had campesino roots, his parents being rural teachers. Thus Torrijos thought and spoke from the perspective of ordinary people who were, in fact, the source of his thinking and authority. As Chuchu says, "his principle source of information was direct experience with reality and direct consultation with the people who were drowning in their problems."[30]

One of the most vivid images of Omar Torrijos is that of him landing at some remote village, descending from his helicopter and talking with poor campesinos. A similarly powerful image for many Panamanians was his elimination of the old elitist Congress, replacing it with a National Assembly of 505 *corregimientos*, small electoral units with one representative from each, including Panama's traditionally marginalized indigenous tribes. Chuchu describes Torrijos' relationship with the common people as one of an "I/You" relationship (as in Martin Buber's *I/Thou*), but in this case expressed through the Spanish distinction between himself as "thou" (*tu*) and the other as "you" (*Usted*), implying his formal respect for the "lesser" person, whether a peasant, poor fisherman or soldier in the ranks.[31]

This personal humility and respect for the poor spelled itself out politically as inclusiveness; an ideological pluralism. Chuchu describes Torrijos as being "*With* the left and *with* the right," not—as one person interpreted this to mean "neither with the left nor the right." Chuchu was quick to add that this did not mean (as in the Spanish idiom) that Torrijos was "neither chicha nor lemonade", that is, someone who never took a position. The same openness prevailed at the regional and international levels: Torrijos had friends who were both on the right and left, which for Panama spelled itself out as a policy of non-alignment.

The real question is, however, did the Panamanian people really follow Torrijos, or was the Torrijos' process really a people's movement? On this matter, even Chuchu equivocates, saying that in the end the people were never fully behind Torrijos, while others charge (more critically) that once Torrijos had the progressive leaders and mass organizations in his movement, he divided them and weakened their grass-roots power. On the other hand, no Panamanian leader in history has ever inspired the people as Torrijos did nor has any person ever had more people attend his funeral than Torrijos. Some analysts also affirm that Torrijos was politically still "in process", learning to confide more in the people and becoming more progressive towards the end of the 1970s. Perhaps, it is accurate to say that Torrijos was the symbol of hope for the Panamanian people even though he was never fully their leader.

These limitations may be the by-product of Panama's colonial history or they may reflect the tremendous pressures he was under from U.S. imperialism. In other words, Torrijos wasn't a dogmatic theoretician but someone who responded to changing reality and his own limitations. Asked if Torrijos was a revolutionary, Chuchu Martinez responded: "more or less".[33] While Torrijos hated dictators (like Somoza) and U.S. imperialism—Central America's two major problems—he wasn't an ideological revolutionary or a doctrinaire leftist. He once said: "It's easy to do revolution in your head; hard to do it on the street."

When Torrijos instituted his democratic process in Panama in 1978, he refused to run for the presidency, holding that his job was to direct the National Guard to be what he believed all true military forces should be: pro-nationalists against both dictators and empires. Both Aristides Royo and Ricardo de la Espriella, presidents of Panama between 1978-82 and 1982-84, respectively, had great admiration for Torrijos as a friend and leader. Revealing his democratic commitment, Torrijos in 1978 said:

> I believe I have my role to play in collaboration with a president and vice-president; there must be a political opening which allows for the inscription of political parties so that the democratic process can go forward; so there can be an election of legislators, deputies, etc. I will use my influence and prestige to convince the military that this is not our moment, that they should remain in their barracks; that our moment has passed.[34]

Torrijos was a realist. That is why he saw the 1977 Treaties as a means not an end. For him, the *end* was not to be found in either the treaties or promises but in the actual removal of the bases. He often said that you can't negotiate a country's sovereignty but must defend it with a gun. Another of his favorite phrases was that one must always negotiate "on your feet never on your knees." This was the source of Torrijos' popularity: *he never capitulated on the issue of Panama's sovereignty.*

But the question remains: what exactly was the relationship

between this important leader and his followers? To find an answer, we turn again to Chuchu who speaks about the relationship and differences between Torrijos and *torrijismo*. For him, Torrijos meant being anti-fascist and anti-imperialist, being in opposition to the U.S. doctrine of national security; to be pro-independence and have good relations with every nation (non-alignment with the super powers); to be in solidarity with those struggling for their liberation and to operate with a new style of diplomacy that was personal, direct and affectionate. Thus, on one occasion, Alexander Haig sent him a note of concern about the presence of a Cuban shrimp boat in one of Panama's ports. Torrijos responded by saying that Haig must have intended to send the note to the Governor of Puerto Rico! On the other hand, for Chuchu, *torrijismo* means to believe in all these things but go beyond them; not to accept (as Torrijos did) necessarily the year 2,000 for the transfer of jurisdiction to Panama; to deepen one's commitments to revolutionary organizations and popular movements. That is, Torrijos was necessary but not sufficient: *torrijismo* can go beyond Torrijos, thanks to Torrijos. Thus in light of Torrijos' death, Chuchu reflects positively:

> The enormity, the magnitude of our failure resulting from his death is, however, less than the triumph to which his memory and revolutionary thinking will lead us. Because they haven't killed General Torrijos; for us they have converted him into a flag.[35]

This vision and fidelity to an image makes it obvious why Torrijos had to be eliminated before any serious anti-sovereignty campaign could begin in Panama. This is why his death on July 31, 1981 was no accident. Furthermore, there had been several specific plans to eliminate Torrijos, with clearly stated intentions to the effect that he should be removed:

- The "Nixon plan" of 1971 to assassinate Fidel Castro and Omar Torrijos, triggered by Torrijos calling on the Panamanian people "to pull the colonial stakes out of Panamanian soil;"
- The "CIA plan" of 1973, reported by an ex-CIA agent who heard of it from the Southern Command, a plan described by

Philip Agee;

- The "Reagan plan" of 1976, which developed out of the *Santa Fe Document* and the publication of Congressman Philip Crane's book *Surrender in Panama*.[36]

It is clear that the pro-imperialist forces wanted Torrijos out of the way long before the Sandinistas became their obsession. But the anti-Sandinista obsession in Reagan was linked to Torrijos because he gave them sanctuary in Panama while Somoza was still in power, as well as sending them supplies through Costa Rica. So Reagan's motivations towards eliminating Torrijos were powerful, not incidental. That is why in the minds of many Panamanians there is no doubt that the CIA engineered his assassination.

Moreover, there is the matter of the manner of his death itself: a mid-air explosion on board a small plane which Torrijos regularly used to fly to Coclesito in a remote part of the Atlantic coast, a trip which only took 11 minutes. The explosion was devastating, clearly the result of a high-powered bomb, triggered by a timing device. As Moises Torrijos, Omar's brother recounts:

> When a plane blows up like this—the word to describe what happened is "disintegrated"—particularly the cabin where the passengers were seated who were turned into confetti, the resulting fire carbonizing the remains. That's how they killed Omar and this is fully confirmed by those who saw it with whom we spoke.[37]

As in the case of the La Penca bombing in Nicaragua, where a highly sophisticated bomb and detonator were used, so in the case of Torrijos' death, everything points to a very professional job and a high degree of sophistication. Regarding the author of his assassination, we know that there high-level officers within the National Guard who worked for the CIA ... including Manuel Noriega. But even if Noriega knew about this plan ahead of time, other actions of his suggest that he would not have done anything of this nature without the CIA's approval.

The most important aspect of the assassination, however, is that it removed the primary roadblock to the rightist forces in the United

States in beginning a process of reversing Operation Sovereignty. Torrijos was Panama's most outspoken advocate of sovereignty and for the removal of the Southern Command from the Zone. This is reflected in his phrase: "Chilean copper belongs to Chile just as the Panamanian Canal belongs to Panama."[38] As in most tragedies there is some irony, so too in this case. Chuchu says, the irony of the Treaties is that in giving the United States the juridical (not moral) right to intervene in defense of the Canal, meant the immediate danger of an intervention was removed. That also implied, however, the "right" to a physical invasion at some later date.[39]

6
The Southern Command: A Hostile Power

Raul Leis, Director of CEASPA, well-known Jesuit sociologist, political scientist and author of *Comando Sur: Poder Hostil.*

Introduction

Just as there were contradictory popular reactions to the passage of the Treaties in 1977—negative for the American public/positive for the Panamanian people—so too, there were contradictory goals in the minds of the two negotiating teams: "In the negotiations, the key word for Panama was *sovereignty* while for the United States the key word was *security*."[41] This conflict of interests was diffused under the banners of Panama's proximate takeover of portions of the Canal Zone, and of the United States' ultimate right to defend the Canal. The fundamental conflict—who would defend the Canal after the year 2,000: Panama or the Pentagon—was not decided. Therefore, in studying the Treaties' meanings, one must keep in mind these two very distinct presuppositions: a) Panama's *political rights* as a sovereign nation versus b) U.S. *military rights* as an empire, with its much larger geo-political interests than in merely a Canal.

What does it mean to say the Southern Command is a Hostile Power?

The Southern Command is a hostile power because it is:

- strategically inserted into the very heartland of the Isthmus;
- intimately intertwined with the Canal installations;
- a belligerent mechanism pointed at Central America;
- structured towards military aggression against the majority of the poor in the region demanding social justice;
- closely linked to the military-industrial complex in the USA;
- a foreign army of occupation with tremendous superiority over Panamanian forces;
- an historic aggressor which has regularly impacted Panama's internal affairs.[42]

Together, these items make the Southern Command a hostile power, a fact now confirmed by the 1989 intervention, as a result of which U.S. troops have directly and publically occupied the whole country! In addition to its role in Panama, the Southern Command has also played an active role in the overt and covert interventions into most of the countries of Central America, justifying Xabier Gorostiaga's thesis that if this intervention is not challenged as unjust and illegal, it threatens the stability of the whole region for the next decade.

The Counterinsurgency Role of the Southern Command

Washington uses the Southern Command as part of its Caribbean security triangle, including Key West, Puerto Rico & Panama. In 1982, the chief of the Southern Command said that Panama "is the smallest but perhaps the most important of the four major commands which the United States has in the world."[43] This military enclave in Panama has its own foreign culture, psychology and idiosyncracies distinct from those of the people of the territory where the enclave is located. This includes both a communications network (radio, TV and press) which are regularly beamed into the Panamanian media and an economic structure which distorts the Panamanian economy.[44] As Gen. Wallace Nutting once said: "the security of the Canal doesn't end at its shores."[45]

The Southern Command is also the logistical center for U.S. counterinsurgency in all Central America, a strategic axis for both military aggression and intelligence gathering. Its anti-communist ideology and aggressive vertical concept of control has produced both military dictatorships and repressive oligarchic governments in Latin America and the Caribbean. Its intelligence monitoring and control contravene the freedoms of all peoples in the hemisphere making the Southern Command a miniature Pentagon, a giant fortress, an imperial vantage point, a hostile power which over the years has constantly changed its form but never its substance.[46]

Removal of the School of the Americas Has Not Diminished the Power of the Southern Command

The removal from Panama of the School of the Americas in 1984 has often been used as an argument to claim that the conditions of the 1977 Treaties have significantly modified the Command's subversive role in the continent. Not only was the Command a structure which pre-dated the School (the Caribbean Command was established in 1948), but the School was transferred on two conditions: a) that it would continue functioning elsewhere and b) that the Southern Command would remain in Panama in force in order to fulfill its "defensive and neutrality" functions. Inside Panama, this includes six military bases and 77 military installations including 11,000 troops (a number considerably augmented since the 1989 invasion). In addition, there is a communications center at Fort Clayton, a satellite station at Telfars, south of Colon; an air base at Howard, a naval station at Fort Amador and an electrical plant at Miraflores.

More importantly, the removal of the School of the Americas has not resulted in any "roll back" of the Southern Command's activities. Gen. John Galvin, ex-chief in the Zone, made it clear that Panama continues to be (for the United States) *the most important country in the sub-Central American region* (as it is called by the Pentagon). It is key in maintaining a U.S. presence in three oceans (Atlantic, Pacific and Caribbean) and in terms of naval flexibility, for as Galvin explains, "only 13 of the 500 ships of the U.S. Armada are too large to navigate through the Canal, so there is no reason to believe that the Canal will be less important to U.S. naval shipping in the future than in the past."[47] Indeed, Henry Kissinger, Secretary of State during the Treaty negotiations, stated:

The new accord places the United States in a much stronger moral and juridical position, in order to defend its interests, than it had in the 1903 treaty.... We will not again have an opportunity to guard our true interests in the Canal under such favorable conditions as those that have been negotiated.[48]

The Role of the Southern Command in the Central American Popular Revolutions

With the advent of the Reagan administration (1981), the role of the United States towards the greater Caribbean region was highlighted by what is called the Caribbean Basin Initiative (CBI), supposedly a project for economic stimulation and development which was highly publicized. *The other CBI*, Low Intensity Warfare (Conflictos de Baja Intensidad) represents the stick in this "carrot and stick" approach to all the countries in the Caribbean zone. These two acronyms are closely linked, therefore, because of the intimate relationships between the economic and military components of Reagan's dream of returning the United States to its power and glory of pre-Vietnam days. And this other CBI is directly related to the role of the Southern Command in terms of curtailing indigenous insurgencies. This led Hugo Victor, a prophetic voice from Panama, to say in 1977: "The Canal Commission will be a dependency, an instrument of the Department of Defense. Panama will continue being placed within the planning and under the direction of the National Security Council and the Pentagon."[49]

What this would imply during the 1980s was a *decade of disaster* for Nicaragua, El Salvador, Guatemala and only slightly less traumatic for Honduras. Honduras would soon be converted into a second Panama, a U.S. "aircraft carrier" for counterinsurgency and *contra* activities. The role of the Southern Command in countering popular revolutionary movements (FSLN, FMLN, URNG) has been key in terms of intelligence, supply and training. In 1984, Col. Edward King, ex-official in Panama stated that the Southern Command "had become a vanguard base structure which allowed it to respond rapidly in case of need" to any place in the region. A year later, a U.S. newspaper analysis stated that the Southern Command, which before was for the defense of the Canal, *"now served to protect the stability of (all) Latin*

America where Nicaragua constituted the principle threat to peace," from the U.S. view.[50]

During his early years in office (1981-82), Ronald Reagan expected an easy triumph over the Sandinistas and a proximate defeat of the insurrection forces in El Salvador and Guatemala. The result was quite different. Not only did the U.S. developed counterinsurgency strategy cause the death of some 200,000 persons in the whole region, close to 2 million people displaced or exiled during the decade of the 1980s, it failed to crush any of the three popular armies. The Treaties of 1977 played a major preparatory role in this Low Intensity Warfare strategy for, as Pablo Neruda described the negotiations: "The demons came together in Panama/where they made a pact of weasels,"[51] that is, how to systematically undercut all resistance in the region.

7
Reagan's Strategy: To Undo the Treaties De Facto

Taken from *Frontier News*, Berkeley, California
from data gathered in Panama by reporter Luis Restrepo

Given the strategic importance of the Southern Command to imperial policy in the hemisphere, it is understandable that the Reagan administration would decide to undo the Carter-Torrijos Treaties. But the question was how to do it, since the Treaties had been passed into law by the U.S. Congress and were approved by a Panamanian plebiscite. As such, they were binding under international law. Any failure to comply with their conditions would be politically explosive inside Panama. So the Reagan administration's strategy was to weaken the Treaties, to debilitate them through non-compliance, to condition their content and modify their implementation. It was a plan that involved defending the Treaties *de jure* while undercutting them *de facto*. Instead of the living up to the "spirit of the law", Reagan's strategy was to respect the Treaties "in name only."

During his eight years in office, Ronald Reagan—through the White House, State Department and U.S. Embassy in Panama—effectively *violated the Treaties in 50 different ways*. First, the Reagan administration forced the passage of law 96-70 which fostered and

justified a controlling position for the United States through "jurisdictional, operative and administrative powers which ... violently disrupt
the spirit and wording of the Torrijos-Carter Treaties."[52] Law 96-70
attempts to perpetuate the image of the Canal Zone by placing it
above the 1977 Treaties. This anti-juridical tactic denies the sovereignty of the Republic of Panama over the Zone territory. Following
are selected examples of Reagan's 50 violations:

1. Establishes a Panama Canal Commission linked to the executive branch, under direct authority of the U.S. President;
2. Reduces the oversight functions of the Joint Board of Directors established by the Treaty to a mere supervisory role.
7. Grants the U.S. Ambassador authority not agreed upon in the
   Treaties regarding the coordination of the transfer of duties
   to the Republic of Panama.
10. Leaves open the possibility that the Administrator of the
    Canal might be an active member of the U.S. Armed Forces.
32. Returned to the USA all possessions and other current assets
    of the Panama Canal Company on the day the Treaty took
    effect.
44. Establishes mechanisms to eliminate positions vacated by U.S.
    citizens for the purpose of not employing qualified Panamani-
    ans, etc.[53] [*Ed. note:* See pp. 163ff.)

Reagan's success in quietly disempowering the Treaties was motivated
by a pro-imperialist determination to maintain the traditional political
and economic structures in Central America through the support of
the Southern Command. Implementation of this role meant "inten-
sification of its spy flights, increased assistance to the Salvadoran
military, direct assistance to the contras operating in Honduras ... all
in open violation of the sovereign rights of Panama,"[54] that is, in terms
of non-aggression pacts signed by Panama with her sisters republics
in the region.

However, Reagan's anti-Treaty success, just as Bush's military
success, represents a pyrrhic victory costing billions of dollars, creating
massive social disorders, economic chaos, mass unemployment and
political repression. The model is a self-fulfilling prophecy: the
Southern Command assures the continuation of war in the region

under the philosophy of guaranteeing peace, for which the Southern Command will *always* be needed (*in perpetuity*). It is the ultimate Pentagon nightmare: in the name of national security, *unending war*!

8
Dismantling Torrijo's Populism & Some Surprises for Washington

Jaime Marques, Simeon Gonzalez & Marco Gandasegui[55], three well-known Panamanian economic analysts.

Behind the scene of Torrijos' political triumph in 1977-78 as the "David of the Americas" (versus the U.S. Goliath), disturbing contradictions were developing which would soon disrupt peaceful Panama as well as produce a series of surprises for Washington. Though Panamanians weren't aware of it at that time, the most serious problem was economic stagnation, a by-product of the worldwide capitalist crisis and Panama's indebtedness. The other was Torrijos' decision to create a "democratic opening" in Panama by encouraging traditional elections and urging the military to retreat to their barracks. This political liberalization—initiated in good faith and no doubt for Panama's good in the long run—would open up a Pandora's box of political intrigue and insider coups over the next five years (1978-1983).

> Just when the negotiations with the United States were reaching their climax, accusations of corruption in the government and National Guard began to surface.[56]

These contradictions, coupled with Torrijo's death, would result in the dismantling of Torrijos' populism reflecting a decline in the *torrijista* project which had been developing for some time due to a complex mix of systemic, personalistic and imperial factors. As a result, Washington assumed that the back of Panamanian resistance had been broken, but it would re-emerge in strange ways and through one of the Empire's own agents.

The most serious of these problems—Panama's growing economic crisis—surfaced at the very moment of the Treaty signing and implementation (1977-78). Known throughout the hemisphere as the "model of accumulation", the Panamanian government was forced to borrow heavily from the banks to compensate for the worldwide slowdown and domestic stagnation, leading to the accumulation of a massive debt. Already in trouble, with Panama owing $1.5 billion, this figure would more than double over the next five years (1977-1982) to more than $3 billion.[57] This indebtedness undercut Torrijos' program of national development which over the years had created 20,000 government jobs, low unemployment, social advantages for farmers and campesinos (in the areas of education and health), and an expanding domestic market. Based on an alliance between the agricultural and industrial elite with sectors of finance capital, Torrijos had been able to manage this by being the government:

> *Torrijismo* represented an alliance between the productive bourgeoisie (agricultural and industrial) and finance capital. This alliance was coordinated politically by the military institution which, at the same time, served as an intermediary between these elites and the popular organizations (workers, farmers, campesinos and small property holders).[58]

The budding economic crisis, which seemed irrelevant to most Panamanians in 1977, became a monumental problem for Torrijos in his last years. Indeed, things became so serious that the government literally "rejected or discarded" the whole Torrijos program![59]

Torrijos' political innovation in 1978—the creation of a "democratic opening"—meant a traditional elite Congress which would replace the more dynamic, populist and broadly representative National Assembly of Corregimientos. In preparation for this transfer of civil power, Torrijos designated his Minister of Education, Aristides Royo to serve as interim president while he also created the Democratic Revolutionary Party (PRD) which would supposedly represent the *torrijista* spirit. Other parties were encouraged to participate, but in 1980, the PRD won 10 out of the 19 legislative seats and Royo became president. But the victory produced a paradox, a handwriting on-the-wall, because most of the 10 pro-Torrijos legislators were from the more conservative sectors of the party. With the death of Torrijos the following year, this conservative tendency within the PRD's own ranks accelerated the process of the torrijista decline.[60]

Torrijos' death would, in turn, lead to dramatic changes within the National Guard, even though his immediate successor, Commander Florez, tried to rule by the book and keep the Guard out of politics. However, behind him (in hierarchical order) stood an extremely ambitious officer, Col. Ruben Darío Paredes, who had even resented Torrijos' power while the General was still alive. After Torrijos' death, Paredes convinced his fellow officers that Florez was plotting with the North Americans against president Royo and on the basis of that accusation had him removed. The move automatically made Paredes the new Commander-in-Chief, to the great pleasure of Washington:

> The populist alliance suffered its first political blow (after the death of Torrijos), from which it never recovered. General Paredes declared that the democratic process would be interrupted and that "real power" would remain in military hands. The United States applauded his words and invited Paredes to Washington where he was toasted by his colleagues in the Pentagon.[61]

The White House and Pentagon saw in Paredes a return to the traditional model of military leader in Latin America where the armed forces govern with an iron hand and serve the mandates of the Empire.

But Washington was in for three unexpected surprises, which emerged out of the contradictions stemming from Torrijos' death. The *first* involved Paredes removal of Aristides Royo—who resigned in 1982, apparently under heavy pressure from Paredes. Whereas Royo represented Torrijos' project of building a *populist democracy* in Panama, Paredes served Washington's goal of recreating an *elitist democracy*. With Royo's resignation, the presidential door was open for Paredes in 1984 since presidents in Panama cannot immediately succeed themselves in office.

In this, Paredes made a big mistake, reflecting his desire to recapture the prestige (of Torrijos), another sign of his ambition. He wanted to be both president and continue managing where "real power" was ... in the National Guard. This was the beginning of his differences with both centers of power.[62]

It was like the Aesop fable about the dog and his two bones. Paredes, holding the bone of Command-in-Chief and remembering how Torrijos was both the military and political leader, saw the reflection of his bone in the presidential waters below and grabbed at that image, in the process losing the military post he already had. Manuel Noriega had convinced Paredes to leave his military post in order to run for the presidency. In doing so, Noriega (as next in the command order) was elevated to Head of the Guard. Later, Noriega refused to back Paredes for the presidency as the PRD party's candidate, so he lost both posts!

The *second* surprise for Washington developed out of Noriega's takeover of the Guard, in spite of the fact that the State Department had good reason to think he would be *their man* in the Isthmus. Given Noriega's long-standing relationship with the U.S. intelligence agencies (CIA and Pentagon), they assumed he would follow their bidding, perhaps (according to some analysts) even turning Panama into the Puerto Rico of Central America, under U.S. guidance.[63]

But Noriega had a surprise in store for Washington: arguing in behalf of defending the waterway, he held that the Panamanian military were in a much better position to protect the Canal against *internal* dangers than the U.S. Army. Towards that end, he called for the old National Guard to be turned into the Panamanian Defense Forces (FDP) and be given increased authority. Initially, Washington was willing to give the FDP certain powers, such as policing functions, crime investigation and social control. But Noriega saw this as a step towards the FDP completely replacing the Southern Command by the year 2,000. Further, Noriega saw it as a means of making the FDP financially independent of the Pentagon. Analysts explain the conflict as a class conflict, but it was equally an anti-imperial strategy:

> The administration of the Canal would give them autonomy from the United States. It would also give them autonomy from the people and the Panamanian state. But by the military placing itself above these national interests, this strategy

clashed with the transnational plan which Washington had developed along with the financial sector and the Panamanian bourgeoisie.[64]

A *third* surprise emerged out of the first: Noriega's plan to by-pass Paredes in the 1984 presidential elections. Noriega wanted someone in that post whom he could control. This subjugation of presidential power to the military did not represent, however, any ideological difference, only the sheer drive for *power* and *control*. Noriega, just like Paredes, Royo and Ricardo De la Espriella (then Vice-President), was fully pro-capitalist, economically speaking. He accepted without opposition all the IMF conditions related to policies having to do with debt repayment. This was even truer of Nicolas Ardita Barletta, who the PRD had chosen as its presidential candidate for the 1984 elections, since he represented the most modern sector of the financial and transnational bourgeoisie. But while Barletta had Noriega's personal backing, he did not have the support of the popular sectors of the PRD, the trade unions and other organized labor movements. Thus, within a year of his election, Noriega was forced to make Barletta step down from the Presidency, enfuriating Washington.

> This move exploded at the end of 1985 because the financial sector challenged such FDP authority, at the same time that that the United States was requesting greater participation from Noriega in its Central American adventures. After Ardita Barletta left the presidency in September 1985, it was clear that the FDP had fallen from grace in the eyes of both the financial sectors and the Reagan administration. The Panamanian military was placed on Washington's disloyalty list ... *it is not by coincidence that the United States begins its offensive against Panama and Noriega in 1986.*[65]

These three surprises—the removal of Paredes, the creation of an independent FDP and the removal of Barletta—upset Washington's neat little apple cart in its strategy of dismantling *torrijismo* and debilitating the Treaties. Unexpectedly, the Washington power brokers had to face the fact that their former agent was now openly challenging their power base: the Southern Command. For all these years, Washington had essentially been using Noriega; now, he was using them. It is important to emphasize that up to this moment—the end of 1985—Washington had never used the charge of drugs against Noriega, even though U.S. authorities knew he was involved in drugs while he was also helping them fight drugs ... typical of Noriega's double dealings. Thus while the campaign which John Poindexter unleashed against Noriega in 1986 was sparked by Noriega's resistance to a more active role for Panama against the Sandinistas, the main concern in Washington was with the FDP's military independence and its projections towards exclusive defense of the Canal after the year 2,000. The State Department was faced by the fact that its *inside informer* (Noriega) had become an *insider traitor*, something the Empire would not tolerate!

Notes

28. Jose de Jesus (Chuchu) Martinez, *Mi General Torrijos*, Editorial Nueva Nicaragua, Managua, 1987.
29. Aristides Royo, president of Panama, speech during Treaties celebration on Oct., 1979, *Panama: Erase Un Pais A Un Canal Pegado*, op. cit., p. 184.
30. Chuchu Martinez, *Mi General Torrijos*, op. cit., p. 63.
31. Ibid., pp. 63-64.
32. p. 87.
33. p. 80.
34. Gregorio Selser, *Panama: Erase...*, op.cit., p. 267.
35. Chuchu Martinez, *Mi General Torrijos*, op. cit., p. 104.
36. G. Selser, *Panama: Erase...*, op. cit., pp. 277-79; pp. 283-286.
37. Ibid., p. 289.
38. Chuchu Martinez, *Mi General...*, p. 98.
39. Ibid., p. 191.
40. Raul Leis, *Comando Sur: Poder Hostil*, CEASPA, Panama, 1985, 2nd edition.
41. Ibid, p. 73.
42. p. 7.
43. Speech by Gen. Wallace Nutting, March 1982, before the Panamanian Association of Business Executives (APEDE), Panama. In it, Nutting affirmed that the United States had enough power to send a force of 10,000 troops to any country in the hemisphere that might ask for help against a foreign enemy, *Comando Sur*, op. cit., p. 87.
44. Philip Wheaton, personal observations on prime time news on Panamanian TV

programs, paid for by the U.S. Army, Feb. 1990.
45. Wallace Nutting, speech cited above.
46. Raul Leis, *Comando Sur*, op. cit., p. 26.
47. *Pensamiento Propio*, CRIAS, Managua, "Panama: Modelo para amar un enclave politico-militar," Edgar Spence, July l989, p. 45.
48. Raul Leis, *Comando Sur*, op. cit., p. 102.
49. Ibid., p. 77.
50. p. 49.
51. p. 50.
52. *Frontier News*, Berkeley, California, Feb/Mar 1988, from data supplied by Panamanian journalist Luis Restrepo, p. 13.
53. Ibid., pp. 13-15 (See *Appendix* for complete list).
54. See *Horizontes*, June 1989, Esmeralda Brown, "La crisis enm Panama," Dover, Del., p. 5.
55. Jaime C.G. Marques, *Panama En La Encrucijada: Colonia o Nacion?*, Editorial Panama, l989, Panama; Simeon Gonzalez H., *La Crisis del Torrijismo Y Las Elecciones de 1984*, Ediciones Horizonte, Panama, 1985; Marco A. Gandasegui, h., *Panama: Crisis Politica Y Agresion Economica*, CELA, 2nd edition, Ediciones Formato Diecesis, Panama, 1989.
56. Jaime Marques, *Panama Encrucijada*, op. cit., p. 36.
57. Simeon Gonzalez, *La Crisis del Torrijismo, op. cit., p. 21.*
58. Marco Gandasegui,*Panama: Crisis Politica*, op. cit., p. 47.
59. Ibid, p. 40
60. p. 25.
61. p. 28.
62. Gregorio Selser, *Panama, Erase Un Pais*, op. cit., p. 270.
63. Jaime Marques, *Panama Encrucijada*,op. cit., p. 40.
64. Marco Gandasegui, *Panama: Crisis Politica*, ibid., p. 30.
65. Ibid., p. 29.

Letter From Graham Greene

Editors' Note: We were pleased to receive the following letter from the novelist Graham Greene, in response to Ellen Ray's "Noriega, Torrijos, and the CIA," in the February LOOT.

Antibes, February 6, 1990

I fully share your feelings about the cowardly invasion of Panama. How will the former head of the CIA, President Bush, now deal with the problem of Noriega and the secrets he knows? He has to be silenced. A proper trial is out of the question. It is laughable to include among the charges the secret import of marijuana into the States when the whole world knows that the biggest grower of marijuana on the American Continent is the States.

Shot while attempting to escape? A little too obvious.

What I foresee is a great show of American justice: a decision that it is for Panama to judge him and not the United States. Let him be handed over to his fellow countrymen now ruled by an American nominee and where the death penalty cannot be ruled out.

You rightly draw attention to the doubts surrounding the "accident" in which Omar Torrijos, a man I knew well and loved, lost his life. One fact is not generally known. According to custom the Canadian builders of his plane sent their insurance company down to Panama to investigate. What was very unusual, the inspectors returned without visiting the scene of the "accident" as they were assured by certain high officers of the National Guard, who included Noriega then connected with the CIA, that the destruction of the plane had been so complete that there was nothing useful to be seen there.

Yours etc,
Graham Greene

From *Lies of Our Times*, March 1990.

U.S. SANCTIONS AIMED AT JAPAN NOT NORIEGA

Analysis taken from articles by Charlotte Elton, Xabier Gorostiaga, NACLA and EPICA[66]

In the pre-invasion history of Panama, where the United States had both motivation and opportunity, the circumstances don't appear to fit the crime in relation to the U.S. economic sanctions. Why apply extreme economic restrictions against the whole Panamanian society in order to force one man out of office? In other words, why use a tank to kill a fly? Quite obviously, because the sanctions were not, in fact, aimed at removing Noriega from office but for another purpose: *the removal of the United States' financial nemesis—Japan—from the Isthmus.*

The crucial importance of the International Financial Center in Panama to economic operations throughout the hemisphere and Japan's massive capitalist investment in Panama, are unknown to most people. In the following brief analysis, we have drawn on various sources, particularly from the research of Charlotte Elton and Xabier Gorostiaga, to flesh out this issue as one of the causes of the invasion.

9
The Crucial Role of Japan in Panama

Last December, Panamanian economist Xabier Gorostiaga presented
the international press corps in Managua an entirely "new" subject:
the role of Japan in Panama and how its interests there fit into the
the invasion scenario:

> The Panamanian political crisis has been used by the United
> States to define North American control of the Canal during
> the next decade and probably on into the next century, includ-
> ing against the interests of its political and economic enemies,
> such as Japan.
>
> Every Japanese press condemned the U.S. intervention
> because it seriously affected Japan's interests in Panama. One
> must remember that Panama is the country with the second
> largest Japanese investment in the world—more than $12
> billion—to be used throughout Latin America, plus six Japa-
> nese banks which were the most dominant ones in Panama.
> Through the invasion, as the culmination of a whole strategy of
> aggression against Japan, the United States has isolated Pana-
> ma, forcing Japan to retreat from its key position in the Isth-
> mus. In the process, Panama has once again become a zone of
> exclusive U.S. hegemonic control.[67]

10
Panama's Unique Banking System

Panama's importance to the financial world has almost nothing to do
with its own internal production or natural resources, except in terms
of its most unique resource, *the transit nature of its geography.* As
such, the Isthmus serves as a "bridge" for thousands of multinational
corporate business dealings and the transfer of enormous sums of
money. Since Panamanian currency is and is equivalent to the dollar,
many banks and other financial institutions based outside the Isthmus
have offices in Panama and use the country as a strategic center for
triangular commercial operations, making huge profits through

avoiding taxes, laundering money (not only in drug transactions) and carrying out accounting alterations on products passing through the Canal, a highly profitable and completely legal operation. By the end of the 1970s, Panama was the fifth largest locus for all U.S. investments in Latin America (behind Puerto Rico which serves a similar colonial function).

Shortly after General Omar Torrijos took power, he created a new banking law on July 2, 1970 called Decree 238, which spurred a rapid and extremely lucrative banking development. Decree 238 created a National Banking Commission which allowed numbered accounts to be set up in Panama, with no taxation on interest earned by foreign deposits held in these banks. These accounts could not be audited nor inter-. vened. As a result, Panama became a huge tax haven rivaling the other world financial centers, such as Hong Kong, Geneva and the Bahamas. By the end of 1973, there were 51 banks in Panama with assets of $1.5 billion; by the end of 1974, there were 68 banks with assets of $6 billion; and by 1988, there were 110 banks with assets of $32 billion.[68] NACLA explained what this financial center implied:

> Essentially, the banking boom has led to the flow of billions of dollars in and out of Panama, but it has not significantly contributed to the economic development of the nation itself.... However, since Torrijos took power, the State has grown as an economic agent. Public expenditures have gone from $65 million in 1969 to $255 million in 1973. Panama's budget in 1973 represented a serious attempt on the part of the government to develop the agricultural sector and improve rural conditions; but the contradiction in this effort is that two-thirds of public investment funds are supplied by foreign financing from the U.S. government and other aid agencies, thus deepening the dependency on these sources of capital and increasing the public debt.[69]

11
Importance of Panama to the Japanese Economy

Within this context, Charlotte Elton of CEASPA in Panama has documented the changing world economic dynamics in light of Japan's rising role in the international finance and how Panama plays into this because of its crucial importance to world trade and finances in the Americas.

During the past five years, commercial exchange between Latin America and the Pacific has been growing faster than Asia's commercial relations with the Atlantic bloc (Europe & the United States). In 1983, Japan began to import Mexican oil, and in 1987 it loaned the Mexican government $500 million to build an oil pipeline to carry oil from the Gulf of Mexico to the Pacific coast to facilitate export to the Far East. Oil is only one factor that makes Japan dependent on long maritime routes for the transport of vital products for its very survival, in which the Panama Canal plays an essential part.

In the world context, Japanese transnational corporations stand at the peak of world power, at the expense of the United States. Of the top twenty banks in the world we see the names of Daiichi Kangyo, Fuji, Sumitomo and Mitsubishi ... not Chase Manhattan, Bank of America or Citibank. In 1983, of the top 74 transnationals in the world, Japan was first with 23 corporations while the United States was second with 21. This absolute change in financial power ranking also implies a relative change for the poorer or developing nations in terms of borrowing and investment potential. Today, Japan invests more in Latin America than does the United States, simply because it has more to loan than do U.S. financial institutions.

This does not mean that Japan is replacing the United States but, rather, that Japan has already inserted itself significantly into the Latin American arena as a new and dynamic economic force, challenging what used to be the exclusive domain of Great Britain and the United States. This can be observed in the table on p. 101.

Next to the United States, Japan is the second largest user of the Panama Canal, the chief financial actor in the Colon Free Zone (in 1984: Japan $313 million; China-Taiwan: $192 million; USA: $172 million)[71] and the most powerful actor in the International Financial Center with 11 banks and $14 billion portfolio, which in 1985 represented 16% of all its banking activities. As a result, the Japanese government decided to make "Panama the center of its Latin American activities" with its national development organization for the Latin continent, JETRO, located there. Prime Minister Yasuhiro Nakasone

Principle Commercial Partners of
Japan in Latin America, 1985
(Millions of Dollars)

Country	Exports	Imports
Panama	3,326	81
Mexico	994	1,870
Brazil	614	1,840

Source: Japan, 1986, Japan Institute for
Social & Economic Affairs, Tokyo (70)

explained this unique situation when he said:

> Japan, as one of the important countries for international
> commerce and as the second largest user of the Panama Canal
> after the United States, has maintained great interest in the
> future of the Canal, keeping in mind its importance in terms
> of its role as a vital connector which unites the two oceans—
> Pacific and Atlantic—in maritime transport and international
> commerce in the world.[72]

12
Between Sanctions & the Invasion ... Japan Is Forced Out!

Against this background of a dominant foreign power operating in the
United States' "backyard", Washington could do little in the financial
sphere: it simply didn't have the money to compete with Japan. But
related to Japan's financial superiority, other social and economic
events were happening which could soon have serious political consequences for the United States. For instance, since 1979, Japan has
been regularly holding financial seminars in Latin America (1982 and
1985), has been giving an increasing number of Japanese scholarships
and has been the key actor in the economic solvency of Latin America, with $30 billion loaned in financing the hemisphere's foreign debt!
Furthermore, in April, 1987, the Japanese government proposed

facilitating another $30 billion in fresh credit to indebted countries in the hemisphere[73], which would have made Japan *the key actor in relation to Argentina, Brazil and Mexico, to say nothing of Central America.* In relation to Panama, Japan has been also been engaged in serious discussions about financing a new sea-level Canal at the price of $20 billion.[74] Any financial countering by the United States was simply out of the question because of its own economic crisis. The only way the United States could maintain its power position in Panama was to reduce Japan's role there or control the rules of the game through its political influence.

The clash that developed between John Poindexter and Manuel Noriega in 1986—which appeared to the U.S. public as a personalistic struggle—must now be viewed within this larger systemic context of power centers: the United States was seeking ways to reassert its dominant world position through political rather than economic leverage. In January 1986, the U.S. press reported that Poindexter was talking about finding an "alternative" to Noriega, but the *Washington Post* never reported the fact that the National Security Council (the agency then headed by Poindexter) had published a background paper on the Panama Canal on April 8,1986 which spoke about *how to counter Japan's rising power position in Panama*[75]. U.S. economic sanctions were initially applied to Panama the following year.

With the U.S. destabilization campaign against Noriega in high gear by 1987, General Manuel Noriega made a trip to Tokyo to discuss the possibility of an even closer Panamanian-Japanese relationship that would have further marginalized the United States. Accompanying Noriega on that trip was none other than Ardita Barletta, Panama's former president and the man whom the United States earlier saw as its chief economic ally in Panama. Following that Tokyo meeting, it appears that relations between Japan and Panama cooled, either because Tokyo perceived Noriega personally as an unstable partner or because pressure on Japan from the United States was so intense that Japan decided to back off. When Washington applied its full economic sanctions against Panama in 1988, Noriega did not seem to be affected in the slightest but the move *did force Japan to begin a massive reduction in its investment in Panama, from $12 billion to $4 billion*[76]. Between 1988 and 1990, these monies were gradually transferred to banks in Miami, Nassau and Costa Rica, while Japan was forced to move JETRO, its development center, to San Jose. With the invasion of Panama in 1989, the United States took over direct control of Panama. Japan must now negotiate directly "with the new boss" on political terms laid down by Washington. This eliminates any possibility of Japanese-Panamanian relations independent of the United States. Nonetheless, Japan's stake in Panama is still very high, so it is not surprising that Japan was the first government to present its credentials to the new Endara government in January 1990. It appears that Japan "will continue playing a specialized role in Panama, but this will not necessarily guarantee benefits for us (Panamanians)."[77] Japan's newly proscribed position in the Isthmus now requires it to operate under conditions laid down by the State Department and Pentagon. As Prof. Gorostiaga warns, this could have serious repercussions affecting Panama and the hemisphere on into the next century!

Notes

66. Charlotte Elton, "El Canal de Panama Y Los Intereses Japoneses en America Latin," CEASPA, No. 6, Sept. 1987, Investigacion PIA, Panama; Xabier Gorostiaga, "La Invasion, el Canal y la guerra fria," CRIES, *Barricada*, Dec. 22, 1989, plus personal interviews with Prof. Gorostiaga by the author, Feb., 1990, Managua.
67. Xabier Gorostiaga, *Barricada*, op. cit, above, p. 3.
68. EPICA, *Panama: Sovereignty for a Land Divided*, op. cit., p.43.
69. NACLA, *Latin America & Empire Report*, "Panama", Vol. 8, No. 7, Sept., 1974, p. 12.
70. Charlotte Elton, "El Canal de Panama", op. cit., p. 18.
71. Ibid., p.8.
72. Ibid.
73. pp. 18, 19.
74. p. 20.
75. Interview with X. Gorostiaga, Managua, Feb. 1990.
76. *Barricada*, op. cit., p. 3.
77. Charlotte Elton, "El Canal. . . ", op. cit., p. 5.

The triumverate sworn into office on a U.S. military base the night of the invasion. Titles are: Ford, "Democracy American Style"; Endara, "How to Speak in Public"; and Calderon, "How to Betray a Country."

U.S. "PROJECT DEMOCRACY": AN ELITIST & IMPERIALIST PLAN

Taken from articles by Marco Gandasegui & Jose Steinslager[78]

13
Defining Terms & Naming the Actors

During the U.S. Congressional investigations of the Iran-Contragate scandal, Oliver North revealed the objectives of the so-called "Project Democracy", the secret name of a clandestine network organized by John Poindexter and Oliver North in the basement of the White House. This project involved exchanging arms for prisoners and using drug-launderers located in Switzerland and other international banking centers to finance the operation. Its purpose was to supply weapons and money to the contras in Nicaragua plus *funds to the political opposition (against Noriega) in Panama.* For these men, the term "project democracy" implied the use of *deceit, destabilization, drugs* in order to force compliance with U.S. foreign policies, all under the guise of promoting the democratic process!

The actors involved in managing this plan, Poindexter, North, Bush, Schultz, Abrams and president Reagan, represent a small, elite group of extremely powerful individuals carrying out a policy without the knowledge of the American public or the authorization of the U.S. Congress. The Panamanian aspect of this project was coordinated by:

Gabriel Lewis Galindo, ex-Panamanian ambassador to the USA and extremely wealthy hotel owner; Ricardo Arias Calderon, head of the Christian Democratic Party and close ally of Poindexter and North; and, Roberto Eisenman, co-owner of the Dadeland National Bank of Miami, implicated by a U.S. federal court for laundering drug money.[79] All three men, ostensibly spokesmen for "democracy" in Panama have three things in common: they are extremely rich, politically conservative and have close ties with the Reagan-Bush administrations. They are members of the Panamanian oligarchy who betrayed their compatriots by selling out to U.S. imperial interests.

In the United States, "Project Democracy" was financially and ideologically supported by the National Endowment for Democracy (NED), which in turn was funded by the American Institute for Free Labor Development (AIFLD), which has long-term connections with the CIA.[80] The primary goal of the "Project" in Panama was to use the democratic process as a means of abrogating the Torrijos-Carter Treaties by putting into the Panamanian government persons sympathetic with and controlled by Washington politics. In February 1987, USAID sent a questionnaire to the principle leaders of the opposition movement in Panama which contained a number of questions all centered on one theme: "What do you think should be done to strengthen democracy in Panama?" The answers came back uniformly calling for *a U.S. intervention of Panama!*[81]

14
Creating A So-Called Democratic Alternative

During the post-Torrijos years, the financial elite linked to the banks and transnational operations gradually replaced the traditional agro-industrial oligarchy led by Arnulfo Arias. Together, these two sectors formed in 1987 an alliance between themselves with the support of the Reagan administration.[82] This alliance had only one enemy: the FDP headed by Manuel Noriega. On June 1, 1987, when the FDP retired Col. Diaz Herrera, second in command to Noriega, the alliance received the golden opportunity they had been waiting for: Diaz Herrera agreed to testify against his former boss. From the base of this insider information against Noriega, the National Civic Crusade

(CCN) was created, which became the political basis for the present colonial government of Panama. During the months of June and July 1987, the Crusade organized street protests and bosses strikes in an attempt to turn public opinion against Noriega.

On October 12, 1987 the Crusade called for an indefinite national strike, but it received very limited popular support, reflecting its elitist leadership and lack of grassroots organization. When the strike failed, the Crusade's immediate response was to call for a U.S. intervention, revealing its fundamentally anti-democratic nature. Other democratic leaders who were neither pro-Noriega nor pro-Crusade, recognizing the collision course the country was on, suggested a transition government—between Noriega and a newly-elected administration—but Washington rejected the plan. In Feb. 1988, the Reagan White House forced Eric Devalle to officially depose Noriega. When this action was rejected by the Panamanian Congress and Devalle went into exile, the United States continued to recognize him as the Panamanian president. Washington them imposed even harsher economic sanctions against the whole country, in addition threatening to intervene. During the following months—March to May, 1988—the Panamanian people woke up every day expecting U.S. troops to be occupying strategic positions throughout the country. In other words, during the months prior to the elections of May 1989, the Panamanian political scene was dominated by the threat of a foreign intervention . . . hardly conducive to a free and open democratic process.[83]

On March 16, 1988, a conspiracy aimed at overthrowing Noriega was orchestrated by the CIA and U.S. military intelligence. At the apparent moment of success, a group of officers loyal to Noriega blocked those collaborating with the foreign enemy. The plan called for kidnapping Noriega and taking him to the United States where a "confession" would be extracted from him in order to demoralize his followers, with the idea of subsequently replacing him with new FDP leaders loyal to Washington. When the coup attempt failed, some of the officers involved in the plot were identified as belonging to Panamanian military intelligence (G-2), long associated with the CIA and Pentagon. The coup proved that Washington's original plan was to maintain the FDP as an organization if it could be purged sufficiently so its new leaders would back White House policies . . . otherwise it would have to go.

15
The Doubly Fraudulent Elections of 1989

The annulment of the national elections on May 7, 1989 did not surprise anyone in Panama, but it did provoke a deepening cynicism about the ability of the electoral process to resolve the national crisis. Faced by the victory of the opposition party led by Endara (PDC), the government (backed by Noriega) had three options:
a) admit defeat before the United States and her internal allies from the Crusade; b) declare falsely that its own candidates were the victors; or c) denounce the foreign intervention of the U.S. government in Panama's electoral process and annul the elections.
It chose this third option. Yolanda de Rodriguez, president of the Panamanian Electoral Tribunal, declared the elections null and void, even though it was clear to everyone that Endara's party, the PDC, had won by a margin of 2 to 1 over the government's party (PDC: 57%; MOLIRENA:28%; Authentic Liberal Party:15%).[84]

When the question of fraud is raised, however, the illegitimacy of the Panamanian democratic process in the election of 1989 becomes a two-edged sword. Clearly, the U.S. government, together with its military and civilian intelligence services, carried out more fraud through its electoral foreign influence, media lying and financial coercion than the fraud carried out by the Panamanian government-military coalition in more traditional ways. The publication *Opinion Publica* ran an important analysis of the electoral process in its June 1989 issue in which it defined two kinds of fraud: *explicit fraud* by the nationalist coalition and *implicit fraud* by the imperialistic coalition: the U.S.Government-Civil Crusaders. Details of the explicit fraud was offered by *Opinion Publica* in 1989 while the implicit fraud had been detailed by *Dialogo Social* in 1988. *Explicit* fraud was characterized by:

1. Alteration of election lists
2. Slow electoral counting process
3. Stealing votes
4. Alteration of electoral reports
5. Manipulation of the media
6. Military pressure and threats

7. Annulment of the election on May 7, 1989. (84)

Implicit fraud was characterized by:

1. Judicial procedures against Gen. Noriega in U.S. courts and threats of extradition;
2. Technical firing of Gen. Noriega by then-president Delvalle;
3. Indefinite national strike by bosses' unions & Civil Crusade;
4. Cancellation of the sugar quota assigned to Panama by the USA and the loss of income and wages that represented;
5. Freezing of Panamanian Bank assets by the U.S. Federal Reserve Bank;
6. Seizure of consular funds due Panama held in U.S. banks;
7. U.S. refusal to pay for the use of the Canal by U.S. shipping;
8. U.S. refusal to present inventories of debts owed Panama;
9. Prohibition of Air Panama flights into the USA;
10. U.S. blocking of IMF re-financing of Panama's foreign debt;
11. Raising U.S. customs costs for Panamanian products entering the United States;
12. Threat not to allow ships flying the Panamanian flag to enter U.S. ports;
13. Threat of suspending use by Panama of its oil pipeline;
14. Aggressive and excessive inspection of Panamanian travellers entering the United States;
15. Pressure by the USA on its allies to impose restrictive measures against Panama;
16. Manipulation of a sector of the International Social Democrats to force Noriega's removal;
17. Organizing street protests and other provocations to create public disorder and thereby destabilize the country;
18. Southern Command carrying out unilateral military operations towards "Total War" without authorization by the Panamanian government as prescribed by law;
19. U.S. conspiring with FDP officers to overthrow Gen. Noriega;
20. Public threats by Southern Command leaders to carry out a military intervention of Panama;
21. The Bush administration's sending 2,000 additional combat troops to Panama specially trained in invasion tactics and using

false accusations against Panama to justify doing so; 22. Inciting ex-president Delvalle and other members of the oligarchy to request armed intervention of the country;

23. Prohibiting U.S. citizens and organizations from paying outstanding bills to the Panamanian government;
24. Various CIA operations aimed at overthrowing Gen. Noriega;
25. CIA planting of U.S. radio transmitter in Panama to broadcast political propaganda against Noriega and the PDC.[85]

Additional foreign manipulation was carried out by the U.S. government through sophisticated propaganda messages beamed at the Panamanian population. The public was asked to vote for what *Opinion Publica* described as a contradiction:

The Civic Crusade/imperialist propaganda declared we had only two alternatives: a) we had to vote because the political crisis could only be resolved through an election, and b) this vote would represent a plebiscite against the Noriega regime. These two objectives converge into a "conscious contradiction" (*inexactitud consciente*). First, because the elections—whoever wins—do not offer an economic model based on our own development but on the rules of the IMF—a model which is anti-national and anti-popular. Since there will be no economic solution to Panama's crisis, no political option representing any true alternative is available to the voters; no real option.

Second, because the May 7 election was not a real plebiscite but it was sold to us as such, we Panamanians voted that way. In effect, they were forcing us *to vote for the imperialist project*. They did this by wedding a plebiscite which chastised a regime which had failed to resolve our basic needs and violated our individual freedoms with a political and economic project that was neither popular nor nationalistic. In this way too, they carried out what can only be described as an *Implicit fraud*.[86]

16
U.S. Crackdown on Freedom of the Press

Under the slogan of "freedom of expression" which is frequently used by the Endara government to stimulate its political clientele in fact has resulted in repression and loss of employment for those newspaper reporters identified with the cause of national liberation. Many of those advocating full sovereignty for Panama, in terms of control over its own territory, have suffered political persecution since the invasion.

For instance, many newspaper reporters and staffers of popular publications, such as *Periodico Bayano, Dialogo Social* and *Unidad* have had their offices searched and personnel threatened. Individual editors and writers, from these and other news publications, have been imprisoned or forced into exile because of threats against their lives.

Particularly disturbing is the fact that 79 out of 300 employees of the *Editora Renovacion,* S.A. (ERSA) had their newspaper rights taken away, posts substituted by others and salaries reduced because their writings did not conform to the official government line or the unwritten rules laid down by the Southern Command about media freedom.[87]

The ex-Director of the ERSa Escolastico Calvo was still in jail (as of May 1990) without any charge by Panama's Justice Department. Other colleagues, such as the leaders of the Reporters Union (Sindicato de Periodistas de Panama): Baltazar Aizpuria and Euclides Fuentes Aroyo were imprisoned by U.S. troops. Immediately after the invasion, the pro-government editor of *La Estrella de Panama,* Panama's leading newspaper, was taken into custody by the North Americans. He was questioned for six hours, warned and then released. From that time on, *La Estrella* reflected a much less nationalistic position and supported the Endara government.

In "colonial" Panama today, even though president Guillermo Endara emphatically rejected the idea that the "accords" signed on May 1, 1990 in Washington, D.C. between his government and the Bush administration weaken the sovereignty of Panama, he admitted that constitutional reforms are being presently prepared.[88] It is clear that "democracy" in Panama will be carefully proscribed by the United States and that Panama's "freedom of the press" will function within defined limits. Just as the new Governors were sworn in on U.S. military bases, so too new fules for foreign relations between the two countries are being written by the Bush administration in Washington, not by the Panamanian people.

Notes

78. Marco Gandasegui, H., *Panama: Crisis Politica y Agresion Economica,* op. cit.; Jose Steinleger, "Democracia, finanzas y cocaina," *ALAI,* Montreal de Quebec, No. 106, August, 1988.
79. Jose Steinsleger, "Democracia," op. cit., p. 8.
80. Ibid., p. 9.
81. p. 10.
82. Marco Gandasegui, Panama, op. cit., p. 50.
83. Ibid., p. 52.
84. *Opinion Publica,* June 1989, No. 17, Panama, "Crisis Politica Se Agudiza Con Anulacion de las Elecciones," p. 3.
85. *Dialogo Social,* No. 208, March-April, 1988, Panama, p. 30.
86. *Opinion Publica,* June 1989, op. cit., "Fraude explicito y fraude implicito" by S.P.J., pp. 8-9.
87. *Periodico Bayano,* March 31, 1990, p. 7.
88. *Diario La Prensa,* May 2, 1990, "Endara: acuerdos con EEUU no lesionan soberania."

PART III

PANAMA'S NATIONALIST FUTURE UNDER THE IMPERIAL EAGLE & REGIONAL IMPLICATIONS OF THE INVASION

The United States seems destined by Providence to plague
the Americas with misery in the name of liberation

—Simon Bolivar

INTRODUCTION: REVIEW OF THE U.S. OCCUPATION OF PANAMA

The Independent Commission of Inquiry on the U.S. Invasion of Panama, which includes such well-known citizens as former Attorney General Ramsey Clark, Graham Greene, Lucius Walker and Dr. Eli C. Messinger, presented an objective report about the occupation of Panama by U.S. forces to the American people on Feb. 8, 1990. The report stated among other things that:

- The Commission estimates the death toll to be between 3-4,000 with the vast majority being civilian deaths. In a recent statement, Panamanian (Catholic) Bishops Emiliani of Darien and Ariz of Colon, charged that 3,000 died as a result of the invasion ....
- It is estimated that 50,000 people have had their homes destroyed, especially in El Chorrillo, San Miguelito, Colon and Panama Viejo. Thousands of others have had their homes ransacked and possessions stolen. El Chorrillo is now completely destroyed. As of February 1, observers in El Chorrillo could still smell the stench from burned bodies ....
- During the invasion, U.S. troops carried out the destruction of almost every political organization's office and records and of those newspapers known to oppose U.S. policy. The U.S. blew up the government radio station while broadcasters were inside.

- The international media was literally locked up for 2 days during the invasion and was refused access to any military operations.
- An EFE (Spanish news agency) photographer was shot and killed by U.S. troops ... and several journalists were arrested.
- Over 7,000 persons were arrested during the invasion. Many prisoners were kept blindfolded for days. This and other violations of the Geneva Convention on Prisoners of War were reported.
- In Santa Ana, U.S. troops barged into the offices of the Youth Movement of the CUNA Indians, arrested its members and destroyed their files.
- U.S. troops had lists of people to be arrested and were dispatched immediately to the homes of almost all prior government, university, trade union, cultural and political leaders. Prisoners were held at Fort Clayton, Empire Range and other U.S. military installations. Extensive physical and psychological interrogations were carried out by U.S. military intelligence personnel ....
- U.S. troops occupied every public building, ministry and university. It is estimated that 10,000 government workers at all levels have been dismissed throughout Panama.
- An intense campaign of vilification and slander has been unleashed in the government controlled press. Ads have been taken out asking people to turn in other people who were supporters of the (former) government .... [1]

Given these conditions resulting from the December 20 invasion, we can anticipate what the immediate future holds in store for the Panamanian people: a society militarily controlled by a foreign army or members of the Public Force commanded by them; U.S. officials who determine the political parameters and economic policies of Panama; a social order where news, individual liberty and political organizing are determined by anti-nationalist philosophies. In effect, Panama has been forcibly turned back into a U.S. colony. As one Panamanian said of this intervention:

How incredibly shameless to argue that they invaded us for our freedom and democracy! Why don't they go and free the blacks in South Africa ... or the dispossessed of their own country? The most powerful military nation in the world, which claims to be the most "democratic and free" country in the West, needed to indiscriminately kill more than 3,000 Panamanians, destroying whatever was in their path, in order to capture one man who was always within arm's reach?[2]

Panama City, Jan. 1990. "The nation is in mourning." "Our popular movement represents a hope of reorienting our people along the paths of true liberty notwithstanding our difficulties." (from *Dialog Social*)

LOSS OF NATIONALISM & RE-EMERGENCE OF PANAMANIAN CONSCIOUSNESS

1
Co-opting Nationalism & Its Re-emergence

The greatest tragedy of this invasion, second only to the massive suffering it caused, was the debasing and discrediting of Panamanian nationalism. On the one hand, the policies and practices of General Manuel Noriega had co-opted nationalism for himself, so that "to be a *nacionalista* was to be a *norieguista*."[3] Therefore, it is understandable that the prevailing feeling in Panama at the time of the invasion was "one of relief—most Panamanians accepted and even welcomed the invasion. There was a widespread sense that all efforts to force Noriega out had failed and that without such an invasion things would have gotten much worse."[4]

But the truth of the matter is that the U.S. government had so exacerbated the economic and political conditions in Panama, deepening the corruption and abuses of Noriega, that it acted as an intimate ally in this process of co-opting genuine Panamanian nationalism. For Washington to present itself as the "saviour" of a "devil" like Noriega is like the stove calling the kettle black. The real tragedy about the pre-invasion process is that it diminished Panamanian faith in their own nation and even in themselves as an independent people. Whereas one Panamanian could say: "When you're about to drown and are being rescued, you don't ask who your rescuer is." Another reflected perhaps prophetically: "I see (this invasion) as a necessary evil.... Right now everybody's drunk (with euphoria), but the hangover's still to come." Indeed, and the hangover of U.S. occupation may last for a long time!

One sympathetic North American priest who served in Panama for several years and visited the country in January, 1990, reflected on this problem of nationalism, saying: "this was one more instance of Panamanians accepting and receiving 'deliverance' from outside; once again they had not been able to forge their own destiny but had the outcome thrust on them by the United States," which means that the "viability of Panama as a nation is much more in doubt than ever before."[5]

Thus the issue of *nationalism* and the Panamanian people's consciousness about their nation and what it will become is now *the key question*, one which will no doubt take them years to work out. Ironically, it may be that the shock of this foreign intervention is what was needed to break Noriega's grip on a false nationalism, so the Panamanian people can begin to forge their own true destiny. This is precisely what the Bush administration does not want ... but it is an opportunity inadvertently given the Panamanian society to weigh their options and clarify their alternatives. The danger they face is similar to the Dominican option back in 1965, an option expressed in Santo Domingo as a result of the U.S. intervention when T-shirts (once again) were emblazoned with a slogan which read: "Get out Yankee ... and take me with you!"[6]

In the beginning, many Panamanians not only accepted the invasion but seemed to prefer a foreign occupation, fearing that Panamanian militarism might reappear. For them, the U.S. forces were seen as the lesser of two evils, as in the popular Kuna Indian wisdom metaphor about rats and the cat:

> It's as if your house was full of rats that ate your rice and bread. No amount of insecticides or traps helped. Since we were tired of the struggle, it was easier to bring in a cat. The cat ate some of the rats but then didn't want to leave and began eating our fish. But if we get rid of the cat, we're afraid the rats might return.[7]

Notwithstanding this attitude, one of the first banners carried by protesting workers read: "The Nation is in Mourning" (*La Patria Esta De Luto*). This slogan inherently rejected the earlier euphoria about the Yankee arrival and expressed a common identification with those who suffered loss from the invasion. A subsequent slogan, "The People Are Discontented" contained a similar sense of commonality but raised to the level of protest, proving that the hard process of recovering their nationalism has begun. As José Martí once said:

> In this world, a lot of damage is done because of cowardice; a lot through indecision; a lot because of governmental promises and imported politics. To cry out with one's country is necessary, to recover the nation through the land and listen to what the land is saying by keeping our souls close to the graves ... for societies move on, they don't go backward.[8]

2
Ongoing U.S. Domination: Removing the Old Leadership

> *The U.S. Southern Command executes ultimate military, civil and legal authority in Panama without respect for the Panamanian constitution or its administrative systems.*
> —Panama Delegation Report, March 1, 1990

> *This invasion has prevented the Panamanian people from building on their own genuine democratic process, representing it as a struggle against the hated Noriega regime. In its place, North American imperialism has violated our principle democratic right—national sovereignty—and has imposed upon us a government which maintains in power the same military leaders as during the Noriega regime.*
> —Socialist Workers Party of Panama, Dec. 27, 1990

When Rogelio Cruz, the newly-appointed Attorney General of Panama, was asked when the local government would take control of the nation's systems now dominated by the Southern Command, he replied:

> Three weeks ago, I was in a meeting when an official from Chepo called, saying that Chepo had been invaded by North American troops. They had entered the Municipal Building and decided to sleep there.... so I told him that if he had an army as powerful as the U.S. in Panama, he should try to oust them at once. What could I do? *We are an invaded country.* That is our reality.[9]

Mr. Cruz again addressed the issue of continual constitutional violations by the occupation forces, when he explained how the chain of command works in Panama today:

> With respect to denunciations, someone was recently in my office to inform me about a certain house with a large stock of weapons and money. So I said: "I am going to order a search." When I called on the F.Q. of the new Public Forces to carry out the raid, he told me that it was necessary to have the approval of Major Manning of the U.S. military.... I didn't know that the Attorney General of Panama needed approval from a U.S. major to carry out such a raid.[10]

As of May 1990, U.S. forces were still holding a large number political prisoners without charges being brought against them. Even a month after the invasion, families were still not allowed to visit their detained relatives. After January, when visitation was permitted, family members had to battle through almost insurmontable bureaucracy to make contact with the detainees. In questioning Panamanians about what they think the U.S. motive was for this protracted detention, one person said:

> Union leaders have been detained in order to pressure their support for the puppet government.... political leaders continue to receive threats that they will be detained.[11]

For months after the invasion, U.S. troops continued to carry out illegal searches including confiscation and destruction of private property on a massive scale, usually on work-related items, such as files, archives and computers. This widespread unconstitutional activity reveals a consistent pattern of intervening in the offices of independent, progressive or opposition organizations: unions, churches, government offices, political parties and human rights groups, including certain embassies of countries with strained relations with the United States, such as Nicaragua, Cuba, Libya and Peru. Similarly, the homes of private citizens who are considered opposition or who hold nationalistic views have also been illegally searched. As in the case of illegal detention, anonymous denunciations—often hinting at the possible presence of guns or drugs on the premises—are used to justify such search and seizure practices:

> The troops arrived. They said that they had received an anonymous call, informing them that there were guns or drugs in my house. Thirty of them, well-armed, surrounded my house and six came in ... and looked everywhere. I was there with young children. Of course, they found nothing. ... [12]

During this same period, U.S. and Panamanian agents—security forces, police and military—carried out an intense campaign of systematic control of anyone challenging the new order, in particular, censorship of the press. Members of the Union of Journalists were blacklisted from their present jobs while those television and radio stations with the most powerful transmitters were taken over and run by U.S. personnel, under the title of the "Southern Command Network."

One of the prominent publishers arrested during the invasion and still in jail is Escolastico "Fulele" Calvo. On the day of the invasion, Calvo's newspaper *La Republica* was the only one to print information about the destruction and deaths and it was immediately shut down by U.S. soldiers. Calvo remains in jail, Panamanians believe, because of his knowledge of the invasion. [13]

In addition, U.S. troops terrorized the citizens in rural areas of

Panama, such as Bocas del Toro, Chiriqui, Veraguas and Darien. Hundreds of troops were reported sweeping the countryside, arresting trade unionists, community leaders, directors of farmworkers' organizations and cooperatives:

> On February 20, U.S. troops conducted another sweep in Baru, in the province of Chiriqui, allegedly looking for guerrillas. They broke into peoples' homes and arrested and harassed members of the banana workers' union. The mayor of Baru fled, and the U.S. officer in charge went to the radio station asked the townspeople to turn him in.[14]

On Feb. 5, 1990, the Independent Commission of Inquiry publicized the fact that the Attorney General of Panama, Rogelio Cruz, had ordered the arrest of scores of former cabinet ministers, heads of government agencies and legislators as well as former Panamanian presidents Manuel Solis Palma and Francisco Rodriguez. The Commission's report contained a list of 74 prominent Panamanians reportedly slated for arrest by the government as part of a U.S. goal *"to destroy the leadership of the political opposition to the U.S.-selected government of Endara."*[15]

This makes a farce of the U.S. pretense of establishing "democracy" in Panama and also proves that the Bush administration has installed *a puppet government loyal to to Washington*. This colonial reality is ultimately worse than living under a repressive regime in Central America, for at least such repression is committed by nationals. Colonialism deprives the people even the right to make their own mistakes, an essential aspect of democracy.

3
Disguising the Colonial Nature of Panama

In one sense, Panama has always been a U.S. colony, dominated not only by the Southern Command but also other foreign enclaves: the Panama Canal Company, U.S. banana companies, the Colon Free Zone, the International Finance Center. The United States has always tried to disguise this colonial reality, proclaiming its respect for

Panama's independence. But its actions belie its rhetoric.

For instance, in the 1973 United Nations debate on Panamanian sovereignty, John Scali, the U.S. representative at the U.N., said that any new treaty should not be "in perpetuity" but have a fixed termination date. He also called for "the progressive integration of those zones utilized for the operation and defense of the Canal into the juridical, economic, social and cultural life of Panama."[16] So much for words. But when a U.N. Security Council proposal affirming Panama's right to control the Canal Zone came to a vote, the United States vetoed the motion. The 16-nation vote was 13 in favor, 2 abstentions and 1 veto ... the U.S. standing alone.[17].

Over the years, Panamanians have lived within a colonial ethos which has produced a sense of powerlessness and an attitude of dependency. One of these attitudes involved what Omar Torrijos called a "waiter" mentality. To explain this term, Torrijos compared Panama with Nassau, as an island of blacks where the tourist trade is the dominant economics and how serving the tourist creates this mental attitude. Chuchu Martinez explains:

> In Panama, we have a mentality of servants, of a *Waiter*. Torrijos said it in English, because Panama is a country of services: it sells water and food to ships which pass through the Canal, it gives Canal services. The General had a profound sense of dignity and with this a feeling that a *waiter* doesn't have dignity or that he has the dignity of a servant, an attitude a person shouldn't have of himself.... [18]

Under Torrijos, this colonial attitude was being overcome because of his insistence on sovereignty and the Panamanians growing sense of dignity which came from standing up to the gringos. With the U.S. imposition of the Endara government, however, that progress has been set back. This setback includes a very clear *racist* component, not only because blacks and mestizos are being fired from government jobs and other positions of influence, but because many of the new leaders and their supporters have strong racist tendencies:

> Endara's only committed support comes from the United States and the *rabiblancos* (white, elitist and anti-populist),

including the old oligarchy, capitalists, nouveau-riche, and military entrepreneurs, who all supported the invasion. These *rabiblancos* have always despised the PRD, which was the only integrated political institution in Panama to offer blacks and mestizos a chance for upward mobility into the middle class.... Notice the skin color of the pro-U.S. revellers: they are almost all *rabiblancos*, who identify most with North Americans, whereas the great majority of Panamanians are Caribbean black or mestizo who were not so enthusiastic about the invasion.[19]

The imposition of a colonial caretaker government has also created class tensions, expressed in a tendency towards retaliation, or *revanchismo*. This attitude is found particularly among the business sector, upper classes and anti-Torrijos/anti-Noriega forces, who want revenge for their years of marginalization from power since 1968:

We repeatedly heard the word *revanchismo*, which roughly means "getting even." The concern is that those who have chafed under twenty-one years of military rule may try to fire many people from government for political reasons and in general go after anyone associated with *norieguismo*, even though he or she has committed no crime. Publically, government spokespersons insist *"Nada de revanchismo"*—No getting even—but not all are convinced. One taxi driver, for example, was commenting that he didn't think it was fair to fire people who had gone to government rallies under duress.[20]

This is why there is rising animosity towards the Endara government, a powerful sentiment among the poor and working classes. An underground newspaper, *El Periodico* expressed this animosity when it wrote about Panama's "national disillusionment," stating that "this *vaina* is worse ... than the Noriega regime,"[21] where the word "vaina" implies being forced into a bind or stuck in a knife sheath, that is, politically immobilizing possibilities for grassroots initiative and nationalistic expressions. One popular newspaper claims that

Endara only has 8% national support (February 1990). Social

discontent has increased impressively, because the people have begun to recognize the great evil and injustices caused by the U.S. invasion and the false promises about reconstruction (by the Endara government). It manipulated the press as the people mourned their dead while reports of scandal, persecution and revenge circulated.[22]

These reactionary examples make it is easy to see why some observers believe that the development of a new nationalistic consciousness will be very slow in coming. Chuchu Martinez has said that unity "has to be organized and involves developing a new conscience, little by little. In the meantime, there will be many bitter pills to swallow, for instance, each time one sees a patrol of soldiers speaking a foreign tongue.... "[23]

4
Robbing Torrijos' Remains To Bury His Memory

On May 1, 1990, the remains of the body of General Omar Torrijos were stolen from the National Sanctuary called the Heart of Mary, a desecration with obvious political implications. Torrijos' remains had been placed in a mausoleum dedicated to his memory located at Fort Amador, where joint U.S. & FDP forces served before December 20. This decision was taken, according to Raquel Torrijos (daughter), precisely because of threats that his ashes might be stolen. His family—Martin Torrijos (son) and Marcelino Jaen (brother-in-law)—denounced the robbery to the Technical Judiciary Police of Panama. The president of the Revolutionary Democratic Party (PRD), Carlos Duque Jaen, said that "the profanation of the crypt should be condemned.... Too much damage has already been done to the country." At the same time, a mural of General Torrijos, located in front of the Patilla Hospital was obliterated.[24]

It is clear that these acts involve more than street vandalism or any personal "vendetta." They appear to be attempts to wipe out the image of Torrijos and with that his memory ... thereby weakening the cause of sovereignty for which he gave his life. Because of the location of the tomb, the vandalism on military property also suggests some official involvement or permission.

5
Emergence of a New Nationalism

The fragmentation of the popular forces in Panama has been one of the main goals of the political powers in control of Panama today, both foreign and domestic. One of their main instruments involves control of the media in Panama, and through it, control of public ideology. Within this pessimistic context, however, *a new nationalism is emerging*.

One of the first protests took the form of demanding indemnization for homes destroyed in El Chorrillo. It occurred when dozens of Panamanians went to the Bridge of the Americas and obtained promises of $6,000 each if they could prove their house had been bombed. An even more important development is the growing resentment towards the ongoing presence of U.S. troops and the feeling that those forces "*in no way represent the interests of the Panamanian people.*"[25] A group, called the Independent Popular Sectors, demanded "the immediate removal of Yankee troops from Panama wthout conditions."[26] This group also listed eleven items as the first urgent steps to be taken:

1. The immediate withdrawal of all occupation troops.
2. Shortening the time-frame by which the U.S. military presence in Panama should be ended as stipulated in the Carter-Torrijos Treaties.
3. Supporting a proper legal process for the detention, judgement and punishment of those guilty of crimes, violations of human rights and administrative corruption of the Noriega regime.
4-11. Demand for the carrying through on various aspects of Panamanian rights, according to Constitutional guarantees, including indemnization and dismantling of the Public Forces.[27]

In this list, the U.S. government is only concerned about #3, having to do with prosecuting members of the Noriega government, whereas most Panamanians see all eleven points as equally important. The courage to challenge the political manipulation of national issues is thus clearly emerging. In February 1990, a newspaper story told about the expulsion of Teresita de Arias (wife of Ricardo Arias Calderon) from El Chorrillo by the women of that poor barrio who had suffered the most from the bombardments. When Dona Teresita came to El Chorrillo she was accused by the female residents "of stealing the limelight and organizing political photographs, trafficking off their suffering and presenting herself as personally pained by the tragedy they had suffered ... so, they told her to get out."[28]

A few critical religious voices are also being heard denouncing the dependency and domination under which Panamanians presently live. For instance, one of the first religious leaders to denounce the invasion was Secundino Morales M., bishop of the Evangelical Methodist Church, who said in a pastoral letter issued on January 4, 1990:

> The country continues to be militarily invaded by the United States, whose troops guard our streets and carry out raids and arrests while developing psychological warfare (together with elements of the new government) to convince Panamanians that the invasion was necessary and legitimate.
>
> We cannot approve of the U.S. invasion of Panama as the way to resolve things, notwithstanding our internal crisis; this occupation is not the way to overcome conflicts between any two nations nor that within a given country either.[29]

In a similar vein, two Catholic bishops, Carlos María Ariz of Colón and Kuna Yala and Romulo Emiliani of Darien, also criticized the U.S. occupation "because it represents a new stage of an invasion by a powerful nation into our society which has traditionally lived under relations of *domination* and *dependency*.... We now seek and in the future must live *according to an autonomy which every sovereign people merit*."[30] The bishops also attacked the witch-hunt and indiscriminate public accusations which now pervade Panama and the fear which the Endara government created by "opposing the rights of the indigenous people to have their own land and to respect their traditional autonomy." While calling for democracy, these two bishops also pointed to the future, towards a *"New Panama."* These gospel signs, they said,

> Make us dream of a new dawn where we can rebuild everything on new foundations. These foundations arise from the oppressed and marginalized peoples. We have to recognize our historical aspirations, respect the indigenous districts, carry out true agrarian reforms and create new sources of work.[31]

In one sense, there is no way of projecting a new nationalism for Panama without dealing with the vision and passion of Omar Torrijos, who once said:

> The truth must be sought directly not in laws, and for that very reason, there is no formula, moral or juridical, that justifies enslaving a person or colonizing a country, just as there is no formula, moral or juridical, which guarantees liberating them. They have to liberate themselves, through their struggles, sacrifices and risks.
> —General Omar Torrijos[32]

At the same time, any new nationalism must move beyond *torrijismo* and its identification with the past military period. Ironically, the U.S. invasion has broken that false link between the Panamanian militarism and nationalism. More importantly, some, like Chuchu Martinez, believe that Torrijos understood this dilemma and wanted the people to move beyond his contribution:

> I am convinced that every Panamanian is a watchman of its Revolution and that each citizen cares for and protects it all cost.[33]

Notes

1. Independent Commission of Inquiry on the U.S. Invasion of Panama, Report, Feb. 8, 1990, New York, pp. 4 and 7.
2. Central American Human Rights Commission (CODEHUCA), *Panama*

Delegation Report, March 1, 1990, San Jose, Costa Rica, p. 18, Doc. #14.

3. American Friends Service Committee, "Panama After the Invasion," Report from a Fact Finding Mission, Jan. 4-9, 1990, Philadelphia, Jan. 23, 1990, p.3.

4. Ibid.

5. p. 4.

6. Philip Wheaton, personal testimony of a Dominican in Santo Domingo, August, 1965, wearing a T-shirt with this slogan.

7. CEASPA, *Este Pais: Mes A Mes*, Jan/Feb 1990-, op. cit., p. 22.

8. *Dialogo Social*, op. cit., p. 26: "Mucho dano hace en este mundo la cobardia; mucho la indecision; mucho la lirica gubernamental y la politica importada. Llorar con el pais es necesario, retorcerse con el por la tierra, y oir, con el alma a las sepulturas, lo que la tierra dice.... Los pueblos continuan: no retroceden."

9. CODEHUCA, "Panama Delegation Report," March 1, 1990, San Jose, Costa Rica, p. 12, emphasis added.

10. Ibid.

11. Ibid., Doc. 1, p. 14.

12. Doc. 24, p. 15.

13. Independent Commission of Inquiry on the U.S. Invasion of Panama, op. cit.,, March 5, pp. 4-5.

14. Ibid., p. 5.

15. Ibid., Addenda, Feb. 5, 1990, Press Contact: Brian Becker, p. 30.

16. Selser, *Panama:Erase Un Pais . . .*, op. cit., p.147.

17. Ibid., pp. 145-146. The countries that voted in favor were: Australia, Austria, China, France, Guinea, India, Indonesia, Kenya, Panama, Peru, Sudan, Soviet Union and Yugoslavia. Great Britain and Northern Ireland abstained.

18. p. 190.

19. Doug Vaugn, "Notes on the Invasion of Panama," Feb. 1990, See: Christic Institute, Washington, D.C.,p. 2.

20. AFSC, "Panama After the Invasion," Jan. 23,1990, op. cit., p. 12.

21. *El Periodico*, Feb. 1990, No. 3, "Esta vaina, esta peor!," p. 1.

22. Ibid., "Endara queda con el 8% de apoyo popular," p. 10.

23. *Pensamiento Propio*, op. cit., p. 35.

24. *El Diario-La Prensa*, May 3, 1990, Panama, p. 11.

25. Communique of the Partido Socialista de los Trabajadores, "Fuera Tropas Yanquis de Panama," Panama, Dec. 27, 1989.

26. Comunicado al Pais de los Sectores Populares Independientes, Panama, January 9, 1990, "El Que Hacer?," p. 2.

27. Ibid.

28. *El Periodico*, February, 1990, op. cit., p. 12: "Damnificados de El Chorrillo Expulsan a Teresita de Arias."

29. Ibid., "Testimonio de un Obispo," p. 5.

30. *Este Pais: Mes a Mes*, No. 26, February 1990, "Mensaje de la Iglesia Catolica Que Vive en Darien, Colon y Kuna Yala," p. 29.

31. Ibid., p. 30
32. Jose de Jesus Martinez, *Ideario Omar Torrijos*, Editorial Universitaria Centro-americana, Panama, 1982, p. 51.
33. Ibid., p. 37.

"The Democratic Revolutionary Party (PRD) will become an active and democratic opposition to the Endara government." From *Dialogo Social.*

ECONOMIC DISASTER IN PANAMA & ITS SOCIAL IMPACT

6
From Financial Crisis to Economic Disaster

As early as 1984, Panamanian financial experts and political analysts were speaking about the country being in crisis, resulting from a combination of the foreign debt and isolation of the Noriega regime. Whereas a powerful coalition of Panamanian capitalists—landed agro-industrialists, transit financiers and independent businessmen, had earlier supported Torrijos, they now turned against Noriega.

Yet, many aspects of the earlier economic crisis were political not economic in nature. About that earlier monetary crisis created by excessive borrowing, IMF policies and the oligarchic isolation of the PRD, one Panamanian economic analyst has stated:

> The the environment and political-economy of the principle international protagonists more than the docility of the national (Panamanian) government in the face of these policies, has transformed the problem of foreign debt into a political problem.
>
> That is to say, the situation of managing the debt ceased being a technical-financial problem; ceased being an economic problem and turned into an *imminently political problem.*[1]

The onslaught of U.S. sanctions and the ensuing invasion turned that earlier crisis of the Panamanian economy into a *disaster*, with devastating social implications. Each of these foreign aggressions against Panama—the sanctions and the invasion—produced *an additional 20% decline in Panama's GNP, for a total 40% fall.*[2] This catastrophic economic depression is clearly the result of outside political decisions not internal corruption or mismanagement.

The U.S. sanctions—the result of political decision by the Reagan adminidstration—included the freezing of Panamanian funds held in U.S. banks, refusal of U.S. companies to pay their taxes under orders from Washington, suspension of Panama's sugar quota and cut- off of international loans and U.S. aid. Domestically, this produced a stampede on Panamanian bank reserves and reduction of domestic demand. Obviously, these internal economic reactions were the result of foreign political decisions.

While there are different ways of evaluating the extent of this disaster ... such as Panama's estimated $10 billion in losses from the sanctions, $2 billion in destruction from the invasion or the present 33% to 50% unemployment, it is obvious that the proposed "$500 million" in U.S. aid will do little to rescue this crippled economy in the short run. Realistic economists in Panama, such as Ardita Barletta, have estimated that recovery will *"require ten years and cost $8 billion."*[3]

Thus, just as the economies of El Salvador, Honduras and Nicaragua were in similar crises in the early 1980s—due in each case primarily to their foreign debts—the past decade of war in Central America turned those three economic crises into disasters, so now the same condition dominates the Isthmus. While initially, Panama was spared the negative impact of the Central American belligerency through its isolation, beginning in 1987 it too became a target of U.S. political aggression, so that over the past three years its crisis was similarly converted inti an economic disaster. Whereas in the first half of the decade Panama's foreign debt was $4 billion, "a figure that represented individually a debt of $2,000 *per capita*, an unprecedented sum"[4], its debt is today estimated at approximately $6 billion, a figure recently confirmed by the Endara government.

7
The Balance Sheet: Financial Debt Vs. U.S. Aid

In addition to the direct economic decline, foreign debt and massive
withdrawal of capital from Panama over the past three years, the
Comptroller General of the Endara government says that another $5.3
billion must be added to the actual total indebtedness, caused by the
massive decline in repayment of personal and business debts, such as
Social Security, electric, water and telephone bills, the drop in sales
and sales taxes, the decline of imports and those tax revenues, and
non-payment of rents and debts from borrowing. In addition, we must
add another $2 billion due to damages caused by the invasion. This
huge loss arose from the looting, decline in sales and the drastic
reduction of foreign trade since December 20. Following is a listing
of the elements of this accumulative financial disaster.

Losses Since 1988[5]

Loss from the Economic sanctions $4,000,000,000
Public Sector losses $5,300,000,000
Failure to pay bills, 1988-1989:
    Social Security $500,000
    Elec,Water & Tel $10,200,000
    Sales & Taxes $1,240,000
    Import Taxes $12,000,000
    Rents & debts $500,000
    SUB-TOTAL $24,440,000
Invasion losses $2,000,000,000

TOTAL LOSSES $11,324,440,000

This total of more than $11.3 billion *does not include the foreign
debt*, but the enormity of these losses places extreme pressure on the
societal and governmental resources, making it doubtful that Panama
will be able to easily return to even its 1987 level of debt repayment
schedules, when debt payments declined.

Against this financial disaster, the question is: how much will U.S.
aid or other short-term financial assistance lead to a recovery from
this disastrous situation? The following listing of emergency humani-

tarian aid, business assistence, escrow funds released and U.S. Congressional grants known to the author are, no doubt, only partial income figures, but they give a perspective on the relative relationship between aid and indebtedness, as of May 1990.

Known U.S. Aid & Escrow Funds Transfers

Emergency Humanitarian & Business Assistance
Housing $22,000,000
Public Works $7,700,000
Small business $12,300,000
SUB-TOTAL $42,000,000
Escrow Funds Released
Usages Unspecified $300,000,000
Projected U.S. Aid Dispersals
The Bush Administration initially requested $500 million which was first reduced to $470 million, and later further reduced to $420 million by the Congress. The Executive branch submitted the following list of needs which the Congress used as a base to discuss its bloc grant.
Private sector Revitalization .... Up to $170,000,000
Govt. Public Sector Invest .... Up to $125,000,000
Intl. Financial Arrearage .... Up to $130,000,000
Public Adm incl. Public Forces .... Up to $45,000,000
Total projected .... $470,000,000[6]
Less $50,000,000
ACTUAL TOTAL AID $420,000,000

This represents a total of $762 million available over the next fiscal year (June 1990-June 1991) in aid and assistance, compared to the above losses of $11.3 billion, reflecting the fact that such aid in itself is not going to pull Panama out of its present disaster.

Furthermore, the policies guiding how this aid is to be spent, underscore the fact there will be precious little of this total dedicated to social relief or welfare. As the Bush administration proposal presented to Congress, its "Objectives of Assistance," place strong emphasis on "sound economic policies," which means: public sector management, financial budget, budget planning and implementation, privatization of public enterprise, trade policy and regulatory policy. Clearly these policies give first priority to debt repayment, U.S. business investment, loans to the Panamanian elite while only minimal assistance to small Panamanian businesses, and hardly anything to ongoing social welfare.

The economic policy of the Endara government around priorities in determining who will receive loans from "business credits" was outlined by Vice-President Ford when he stated that "this is going to be a country that is 100% private enterprise."[7] Coupled with that philosophy is the Republican position, presented by New York's Senator Alfonse D'Amato in an article entitled "To Build a Free Panama: Privatize."

> The new government should embark on a bold, creative program of *privatization*, to demonstrate to international markets its commitments to economic freedom.
> Another obstacle to economic prosperity in Panama is the insidious cradle-to-grave social welfare system, which extends deep into the private economy. Panama's inflexible labor code makes dismissal of unproductive workers nearly impossible. As a result, high labor costs have driven thousands of jobs to nearby countries, adding to Panama's economic dislocation.[8]

This *privatization* philosophy implies driving the final nail into the coffin of the progressive policies of the Torrijos regime in terms of Social Security benefits, on-the-job protection, retirement benefits, etc., many of such benefits that are taken for granted in the United States. This will create particular hardships on those newly fired as well as the chronically poor, the latter presently estimated as 40% of the population. This is why thousands of Panamanians have taken to the streets, publically challenging D'Amato's policy, saying *"No to Privatization."*[9]

8
Social Impact of the Economic Disaster

Panamanian economists and sociologists alike agree that the overall impact of the U.S. sanctions and invasion spell social disaster for tens of thousands of marginal and unemployed Panamanians. In addition to the overall decline of 40% in the GNP and the income reductions and price rises which have resulted, this disastrous depression has created mass unemployment. Whereas by November 1989 (before the invasion), it is estimated that 35% of the work force was out of a job, today the figure is as high as 50% among certain social sectors and in some geographical areas, with urban employees particularly hard hit. One of Panama's noted sociologists, Marco Gandasegui, points out that

> The effects of the sanctions can be measured quantitatively and qualitatively. Unemployment increased by 50% in the period from March to November (1988). The government's collection of funds decreased by 50% and the GNP decreased by 20 percent. This meant that health centers were without medicines, schools without supplies, highway infrastructure was deteriorating, industry was stalled and construction paralyzed.... The psychological and moral affects caused by the U.S. sanctions have had a tremendous (negative) impact on the state of the Panamanian nation. People feel defenseless and without any international solidarity.... According to official calculations, the U.S. aggression (from the sanctions alone) has caused a massive expulsion of more than 100,000 salaried persons from the "modern sector of the economy."[10]

Then came the invasion, causing immediate unemployment for 5,000 more who lost their jobs as a direct result of the looting, to say nothing of the thousands laid off from government jobs as a result of IMF and Endara policies. The combined social impact of these developments—two sanctions, invasion and austerity policies—have created an extremely unstable society in Panama today, characterized by:

- Rising theft of both businesses and private homes;[11]
- Significant escalation in the prison population and escapes;[12]
- Growing social and labor protests from job & housing losses[13]
- Increased societal tension, recrimination and a significant rise

in the number of private citizens carrying guns.[14]

These social repercussions have created negative attitudinal and psychological changes in the Panamanian people, who up to 1987 were a relatively easy-going, cultural adaptable and non-violent people. Today, many Panamanians feel afraid, embittered, revengeful and as one person said: "on their own." This social interplay between imposed U.S. policies and Panamanian attitudes has created new social tensions and class animosities. As a result, resentment that was previously focussed on Noriega and his arbitrary military rule has now shifted against the Endara government and U.S. occupation forces.

9
Questionable Financial Background of the New Governors

Criticism of a number of the highest officials in the Endara government has arisen not only because of its colonial subservience to Washington, but from the elitist attitudes and the economic history of these men. A number of newspaper articles have expressed public cynicism about the new government, saying: "we know who you are." For instance, they know the financial background of these new colonial governors and the fact that

- *Guillermo Endara* was a director of the Banco Interoceanico, identified by the Drug Enforcement Administration's trials as a source for drug money laundering;
- *Guillermo (Billy) Ford* is part owner in the Dadeland Bank of Florida, linked to the Medellin Cartel;
- *Rogelio Cruz*, the new Attorney General, is director of the First Interamericas Bank, directly linked to the Cali drug operation;
- *Ricardo Arias Calderon* is also linked to these banks as is his finance minister, Mr. Galindo.[15]

In addition, personal images of the new government have made people sceptical of its good will and sincerity. For instance, during president Endara's fast, he made it very clear that it was not meant as a criticism of the Bush administration but only to emphacize Panama's need for money. But Endara's claim that he was only fasting out of sympathy for the suffering of Panama's poor was mocked by many, not only because he is extremely fat reflecting his soft lifestyle, but also because during the fast he admitted he is a person with a taste for "exquisite foods."[16] At that very moment, CARITAS was feeding 30,000 people a day in Panama at its soup kitchens.

In January 1990, it was estimated that 44% of all Panamanians lacked enough money for basic food, housing and health needs. When the new U.S. Ambassador to Panama, Deane Hinton, repeatedly asked the people "to have patience"[17] about the U.S. aid which was surely coming, many Panamanians were furious. Some five months have passed since the invasion and still no assistance from Washington. Many people sked: how long can families with unfed children and rents unpaid continue to be patient?

Therefore, just as the removal of Noriega is not going to solve Panama's economic crisis neither is U.S. aid. The economic price the Panamanian people have had to pay for Washington's stated objective of removing Noriega from power has been tremendous. While the Bush administration has won a short-term political victory in Panama, the social suffering it has caused will last a long time. This dynamic creates precisely the opposite situation from what Washington wanted in Panama: an unstable social and economic environment.

Notes

1. Gomez & Salazar, *Panama 1988*, "Panama: Que Hacer Con la Deuda Externa?" by Prof. Jose A. Gomez P., Panama, 1988, p. 54.
2. Marco Gandasegui, *Panama: Crisis Politica y Agresion Economica*, CELA, 2nd ed., 1989, p. 47.
3. *Dialogo Social*, Feb/Mar 1990, op. cit., p. 31.
4. Gandasegui, *Panama: Crisis Politica, etc.*, op. cit., p. 40.
5. *Dialogo Social*, op. cit., pp. 29-30.
6. Foreign Assistance Act, Fiscal 1990, U.S. Congress, Sec. 2: "Assistance for Panama," Appropriations Committee, U.S. House & Senate.
7. *Dialogo Social*, op. cit., p. 29.
8. Commission on Inquiry, op. cit., March 5, 1990, Addenda, p. 8, "To Build A Free Panama: Privatize!"

9. *Dialogo Social,* op. cit., p.14, See: graphic.
10. Marco Gandasegui: *Panama: Crisis Politica, etc.,* pp. 56-57.
11. Philip Wheaton, personal testimony from friends in Panama & Colon, Feb. 1990. Note: this phenomenon of petty thievery has increased significsantly since February, according to official reports.
12. CODEHUCA Testimonies; Commission of Inquiry; *Dialogo Social,* op. cit., p.17: "An official of the Model Prison explained that after conversations which visitors had with prisoners where 'promises difficult to keep were made, a great riot occurred among the prisoners, some began banging on the doors of their cells and one gave way, allowing them to escape.' Some 50 prisoners escaped; 15 were later captured."
13. Commission of Inquiry, op. cit., March 5, 1990, p. 6: "300 persons whose houses were destroyed blocked the Bridge of the Americas for more than four hours, demanding indemnization from the U.S. government." Also, "500 El Chorrillo residents occupied a building under construction and demanded the U.S. send money to finish it and allow the people to live in it."
14. Philip Wheaton, personal testimony received from people living in a well-to-door neighborhood as a personal witness of what they had seen occur. Feb. 1990 in Panama City.
15. Commision of Inquiry, op. cit., Feb. 8, 1990, p. 10.
16. *Barricada,* Managua, Nicaragua, March 4, 1990, p. 12.
17. *Ibid.*
18. Commission of Inquiry, op. cit., Feb. 8, 1990, p.10.

Colonial president of Panama Guillermo Endara—a man without any political party.

INVASION REALITIES: DECEPTION, UN-CONSTITUTIONALITY, TOTAL WAR, SYMBIOSIS AND ARROGANCE

> *Panamanian People: you have been deceived. And now only one recourse remains: that this generation offer its life so that other generations will find here a free nation.*
> —Omar Torrijos, 1971

Deception of the people who are citizens of a victim nation by U.S. propaganda is only part of the picture of the Panamanian invasion, the other side involves the deception of the American public. The invasion scenario is a perfect case study in how such deception operates. One of the strangest aspects of the invasion dynamic involves the October 1989 coup attempt against Manuel Noriega and how he was able to escape from his capture.

The explanation involves a carefully planned U.S. covert operation aimed at *not supporting the coup attempt and setting up the conditions that would justify the invasion.* The coup itself was a desperate effort by certain Panamanian Defense Force officers to head off the planned invasion. According to *Unclassified,* newsletter of the Association of National Security Alumni, "the coup leaders thought that by handing over Noriega, the invasion with all its destructiveness including the destruction of their institution, would be avoided."[1]

The order to invade Panama had been given to General Thurman by Pentagon officials the previous July (1989), but that decision needed justification before the December operation would be acceptable to the U.S. Congress and American public. That is why the Southern Command failed to block the route over which the battalion loyal to Noriega moved to crush the revolt. The reasons *Unclassified* gives for Washington not allowing the coup to succeed include:

- To give President Bush the military victory he needed to destroy the wimp image that plagued him;
- To allow the U.S. Special Operations Command to demonstrate its prowess in combat;
- To show the need for a big combat budget even in the absence of any continuing threat from the Soviet Union;
- To warn all Third World countries what the United States will do in response to any military resistance to its domination;
- To put down any resistance from Congress to military decisions made by the Executive and Pentagon.

In order to carry out this strategy, however, more was required than simply freeing Noriega and scap-goating him. The invasion had to be justified by aggressive incidents, supposedly carried out by the Panamanian Defense Force. *Unclassified* explains how these incidents occurred really occurred and involved U.S. not Panamanian forces:

> (U.S.) General Lindsay, sometime soon after September 11, sent one of the Army's secret Delta Force teams into Panama ... this team was responsible for many of the "incidents" involving firing at U.S. forces and "penetration" of U.S. installations, alledgely by Panamanian troops ... cited as provocations by "Operation Just Cause." Referring to the Nazi use of staged provocations to justify its attack on Poland in 1939 ... "We Polanized Panama."[2]

Not only were Panamanians deceived but the American people as well. The deceit did not involve General Manuel Noriega but the imperial warmongers in Washington. Omar Torrijos' warning to the Panamanian people is just as applicable to the U.S. public: *"You have been deceived."*

10
Illegality & Unconstitutionality of the Invasion

In his analysis of the illegality of the Panama invasion, Gary M. Stern, talks of how *"Bush's War Powers Shuffle Fails to Satisfy the Constitution"*:

> We have indited drug narco-terrorist in Colombia and Bolivia and in other countries and the President (Bush) says, when asked why we do not go in and get them, that we have no constitutional authority to do that, and he is right. . . . He has no constitutional authority to do that. . . .
>
> So to reaffirm such an authority (as in the case of Noriega) is a fundamentally unsound constitutional notion *because there is no such authority under the Constitution*.(1)

Amidst the clamor of support by Washington policy-makers for the U.S. invasion of Panama, little was said about whether the action was lawful. While a number of people raised objections to it on the basis of international law (*New York Times*, 1/10/90), far fewer questioned whether the President had the legal authority to launch the invasion under the U.S. Constitution. *Clearly, he did not.*

Shortly after December 20, Bush quietly submitted a report to Congress explaining the legal authority for the invasion and the estimated scope and duration of our involvement. The President's note stated he was submitting the report "consistent with" the War Powers Resolution rather than "pursuant to" it because he, like all presidents before him, knows the law is unconstitutional.

But the War Powers Resolution is unconstitutional for a different reason than the one Bush presented, namely, because it grants him more power than the Constitution itself allows. Thus, in filing his report, the President subtly danced around one of the most vexing legal and constitutional issues of the day: the power to declare war.

While the Constitution says precious little about the war power, what it does say is quite simple: *Congress* shall have the "power to declare war"; the President is the "Commander in Chief" of the armed forces, but only Congress can decide to commit the United States to a foreign military action. Once the decision is made, then the President is fully empowered to execute it. He can act without congressional authorization only in emergency circumstances to defend the United States when it or its armed forces have been attacked or to rescue or protect U.S. persons abroad, and then only to the limited extent of defending troops, performing a rescue or leading Americans to safety.

Contrary to President Bush's assertions, *Panama was not such an emergency situation*, nor did the circumstances entitle him to conduct an invasion to depose a foreign leader or to implement a treaty without Congressional authorization. To the extent that American soldiers were under attack and American civilians were in danger, the President had the authority to protect those lives; but he should not have used those circumstances to justify a full-scale invasion and overthrow (a government) without the prior authorization of Congress.... [2]

In a separate analysis on *proportionality*, Doug Vaugn—a U.S. expert on Panama—explains how in international law, any belligerent response must wait until the aggressor nation has acted, and then, the response must be in proportion to the initial aggression.

International law, whether under the United Nations Charter or the Rio Treaty of the Organization of American States, only allows one nation to invade another in self-defense against a real threat. There was no real threat by Panama against the United States. Even in the presence of a real threat, military action is only permitted after exhausting all peaceful means for redressing the grievance, including appeals to the OAS or World Court. In the case of the U.S. invasion of Panama, the OAS repudiated Washington's action. Even our puppet allies in El Salvador and Honduras abstained, refusing to vote with the United States on principle. During the Reagan administration, the United States had similarly flouted the judgement of the World Court in the case of foreign aggression by the U.S.-backed contras in Honduras brought by the Sandinista government. In the Panama case, even assuming a real threat and the exhaustion of other alternatives, violence carried out in self-defense must be proportional to the injury suffered by the other nation, under the treaties in question.

Clearly, U.S. violence against Panama was totally out of proportion with any so-called violence by Panama against the United States.[3]

The Panama Canal treaties give the United States the right to intervene in Panamanian affairs *only if the Canal is endangered*. The Carter-Torrijos Treaties give no justification, however, for the kind of invasion which the U.S. government mounted and indeed limit any intervention there to certain defined areas under joint U.S./Panamanian jurisdiction, and then only if the Canal is endangered.

For the Bush administration to claim that Panama had declared war on the United States is a fabrication, or at best, an egregious exaggeration. What the National Assembly of Panama did say was that the United States *was behaving as though a state of war existed between the two countries*, referring to four U.S. aggressive acts:

1. U.S. economic sanctions, amounting to a blockade of Panama.
2. U.S. plans to kidnap or remove its military leader.
3. U.S. coordinated *coup d'etat* against Manuel Noriega.
4. U.S. military maneuvers on Panamanian soil with the stated intent of preparing for an invasion.

Therefore, *it was the United States that declared war on Panama not the other way around.* While Panama's National Assembly gave General Noriega certain limited powers to deal with this crisis, it was Washington that took the initiative in the aggression.

11
Total War Elements:
Absence of Inter-American Collaboration

Not only did the OAS condemn the U.S. invasion and call for an immediate withdrawal of its troops from Panama, but for the first time, Washington failed to consult with its inter-American allies concerning any joint military collaboration. Unlike the case of the Dominican Republic in 1965, where an inter-American peace-keeping force was brought in after the fact (i.e., Brazilian troops), or in the case of Grenada, where five Caribbean governments were pressured by the United States into signing a document approving the 1983 invasion, subsequently using police forces from Jamaica and Barbados to reinforce its own troops.

In the Grenada invasion, the United States did employ, however, various tactics that were then repeated in Panama which appear to constitute elements of what is now called "total war" strategy:

a. Long-term psychological preparation of the American public playing on their fears of communism in the Caribbean;
b. Barring U.S. press from the island during the first days of the invasion to prevent them from reporting the horrors of the action ... and then totally controlling the local media and foreign reporters about what was happening;
c. Insisting there had been no civilian casualties though many Grenadians did die, such as those killed by the U.S. bombing of a civilian hospital;
d. Official deception about the realities of life in Grenada and the threat to American lives, presenting the invasion as a rescue mission of the students at St. George's medical school who were under no threat.[4]

In addition to these four characteristics, various new elements were added in the case of the invasion of Panama:

e. It was an exclusively U.S. military action with no involvement of other hemispheric forces nor collaboration with regional governments;
f. The justification for this invasion not to save American lives or to fight communism but supposedly to prevent drugs from the entering the USA, a new U.S. rationale for intervention;
g. Use of highly sophisticated weapons and aircraft, testing many of these under combat conditions for the first time, and using totally excessive fire-power as if in preparation for future wars since they represented what many witnesses characterized as overkill given the nature of Panamanian resistance;
h. Extensive and efficient clean-up operations of both bodies and buildings in order to hide the evidence of the invasion's impact

from foreign reporters and the Panamanian public.

When we put these items from U.S. invasions of Grenada and Panama together, they appear to be an outline for what we have called the *total war model*; the Pentagon's strategy for quick and decisive interventions against Third World nations when the circumstances are propitious. This model represents an alternative to the Vietnam syndrome and the "low intensity warfare" carried out in El Salvador, both viewed as relative failures because of their duration, loss of life, inconclusive results and lack of civilian support. "Total War" therefore appears to be a more acceptable format from the Pentagon and U.S. media perspective and correspondingly more ominous for any independence or liberation process in the hemisphere during the next decade.

12
Symbiosis between the Empire & Noriega

Is the Bush's dance with Noriega over? *No* ... because their relationship is symbiotic: they need each other. When we look at who Noriega was and what he did, we are looking at the mirror image of how U.S. imperialism functions in the Third World. Many analysts think that a deal may have been struck between Washington and Noriega during his asylum in the Apostolic Nuncio's residence last January. They project that after a long, drawn-out trial in which Noriega is smeared even more, further justifying the invasion, that he will be let off on a technicality (the illegality of his extradition from Panama) and will end up in some foreign country discredited but free.

The reason this macabre U.S./Noriega dance goes on is not because of the trial, however, but rather because *norieguismo* is an *imperial way of life*. Whether the U.S. dancing partner is Rios Montt, Napoleon Duarte, Suazo Cordova, Cristiani, Duvalier or Marcos ... the empire uses such puppet leaders—military and civilian—for its hegemonic purposes, manipulating such leaders for a time and then discarding them. Who is guilty of sin when a married man of means calls up a high-priced prostitute while on a business trip in some strange place? The answer is *symbiosis*: they both are. They use each other, both prostituting the other for personal reasons. Such is the nature of U.S.imperial policy. If we hold up the misdeeds of Noriega, behind many of them we find the smiling face of Uncle Sam.

Consider just two examples, both of them recently publicized in an article on Noriega in *Newsweek:*

> *First* . . . Manuel Antonio Noriega was born in poverty in 1934. He was illegitimate, his mother put him in a foster home when he was five. 'Noriega's teenage ambitions, according to his school yearbook, were "psychiatrist" and "president of the republic."
>
> Instead, a scholarship landed him in a military college in Peru. He allegedly worked for the CIA while at school, supplying information on suspected leftists among his fellow cadets. . . .
>
> Noriega entered the National Guard after graduation and was posted as a junior officer to Colon province, where he allegedly raped a prostitute. A rising young officer named Omar Torrijos kept him from being punished and sent him to Chiriqui, where he raped a 13-year-old girl and Torrijos again intervened.
>
> Torrijos took power in Panama in a 1968 coup, and young Noriega soon repaid him for his past protection. A group of officers attempted to overthrow Torrijos while he was out of the country (in Mexico). Noriega, then in charge of Chiriqui province (in David) secured an airstrip so that Torrijos could return safely and squash the coup. A month later, Noriega ascended to the rank of Lt. Col. and head of what was then the National Guard's G-2 section. This gave him control over military intelligence. . . . [5]

What *Newsweek* conveniently leaves out of this narrative is that before this event and before Noriega ascended in rank, he had been a CIA agent. When the telephone call came from Torrijos about whether it was safe for him to return to Panama (in 1969), Noriega *first called the CIA and got permission from them to let Torrijos back in the country!* No doubt Washington assumed that Torrijos, as a Panama strongman, would become in time yet another typical Central

American military officer who would do its bidding. *Newsweek* also fails to mention the fact that from that time on, Noriega became the chief source of information for both the CIA and Pentagon intelligence ... for pay and favors! And so the dance goes on....

> *Second* ... According to a former top aide to Noriega, Jose Blandon, the Panamanian strongman met secretly with Lt. Col. Oliver North in 1985 aboard Noriega's yacht. The two men hatched a scheme to frame the Sandinista government of Nicaragua before a congressional vote on resuming aid to the contras. European middlemen would purchase East German automatic rifles and grenade launchers and ship them on a Danish freighter, the Pia Vesta, via Panama to El Salvador. There, the Salvadoran military would "intercept" the weapons, claiming Managua intended them for leftist guerrillas (the FMLN). According to Blandon, the plan fell through in June 1986 when the *New York Times* implicated Noriega in drug trafficking. Enraged, Noriega took custody of the ship and its $26.5 million cargo.
>
> David Duncan, the Miami-based arms dealer who handled the weapons aboard the Pia Vesta, claimed the East German arms were bought with part of the $26.5 million payment Pretoria made to a group of European businessmen.... According to documents turned up by the congressional Iran-contra investigation, the late CIA director William Casey sought South African assistance in early 1984, as Congress was moving to shut down covert CIA aid to the contras.
>
> Duane Claridge, the CIA official who ran the Nicaraguan project for Casey, testified that the South Africans were reluctant to deal with the contras directly, but suggested they might provide aid to a third country to help it train and equip the Nicaraguan rebels.... [6]

Such was the nefarious symbiotic relationship between Noriega and high officials of the U.S. government. In this case, *Newsweek* fails to say that the drug charges against Noriega were used by John Poindexter because Noriega wouldn't go along with *all* the U.S. machinations in Central America. Whereas *Newsweek* labels the above story as a "masterpiece of double-dealing," what it is in fact is a *double betrayal*: Noriega betraying the Panamanian people and the CIA and NSC betraying the American public ... each out of their separate motivatios and each justifying their particular forms of prostitution for "higher" causes.

13
Imperial Presumptuousness Vs. Panamanian Integrity

Any reflection on the future of Panama's nationalism must begin with a look at the presumptuousness of U.S. imperial policy makers. On the one hand, it is clear—as Xabier Gorostiaga said last December—that Panama was "a clean flag in dirty hands" (referring to Noriega), but that flag has been even more gravely sullied through the U.S. invasion and its occupation. Even more serious is the U.S. imperial presumption that certain leaders have the right to do what they wish with Panama.

For example, last August (1989), General Marc Cisneros, chief of the Southern Command, stated that he believed a U.S. military intervention into Panama "would pass as an event of little importance" because the majority of Latin Americans, he said, "would applaud our action." In his macho military manner, General Cisneros dismissed any resistance by the OAS and justified the U.S. military maneuvers which he was directing at that time in Panama against towns near the Canal in the name of defending the waterway, adding: *"We don't need any permission from the Panamanians"*[7]

Another person who has spoken out on Panama is Roger Fontaine, co-author of the *Santa Fe Document* and leader of the Council on Inter-American Security. While he admits that the U.S. invasion has done serious damage to stability and democracy in Panama, his realism fails to disguise the same imperial arrogance:

> Although it cannot be proved, there is also a sense of hubris in all this. Perhaps, American officials thought that after shoe-horning from power the likes of Ferdinand Marcos in the Philippines and Haiti's Jean Claude Duvalier (Ed.: leaders whom Washington supported both financially and ideologically

for years), Noriega would surely understand that once the United States had decided the dictator must go, he should have *the common courtesy to pack his bags and leave!*

But the overthrowing of Noriega hardly ends Panama's problems. The focus on Noriega as the problem has ill-prepared both Panamanians and Americans for the tasks and burdens ahead.

The prospect of an unstable or unfriendly regime in Panama at the end of the century is not an inviting one.... To prevent that from happening will require time, patience, money, luck and above all, commitment. All of the above are extremely scarce resources in Washington as our policy in Panama has so aptly demonstrated in the last few decades....

As U.S. officials discovered belatedly, economic sanctions were not surgical strikes on Noriega at all, but very blunt instruments *which punished the Panamanian people more than the regime.*

Moreover, the use of U.S. military force to destroy the Noriega regime has had the effect of once again having the Americans solve Panama's problems and not the Panamanians. *Dependence on the United States thus has increased, not diminished,* complicating the problem of Panamanian stability....[8]

While these insights are accurate, they reflect why U.S. strategists working on Panama are uneasy. This probably explains why as late as March 1990, Southern Command troops were still making military sweeps through various Panamanian departments far from the Canal Zone. This is also why unknown forces recently removed the ashes from General Omar Torrijos' grave.[9]

Any expression of nationalism—from the living or the dead—is seen as potentially subversive and Omar Torrijos continues to be a powerful symbol even from his grave. Memories of his adamant position on sovereignty remain with the Panamanian people as an inheritance for the future, as reflected in these words:

- North Americans generally consider all those who defend themselves against U.S. attacks as aggressors.[10]

- Together we will conjugate the verb "decolonize" not in letters but in action, knowing that our People have learned to write their ABCs of liberty not with ink but with blood.[11]

First Steps Into the Future:
Patriotism, Solidarity & Unity

Many questions remain about Panama's future. In light of the imperial forces now controlling its territory, the forging of a new nation will require a unique combination of those real yet mythical factors: *patriotism, solidarity* and *unity*. These elements are already emerging through new voices from Panama, Mexico and the United States which reflect the ongoing *honesty, love* and *fraternity* in the Americas.

The *honesty* of the human rights organizations in Costa Rica and Panama have done more to explode the lies and myths of the U.S. invasion than any other single group. The Commission on Human Rights for Central America (CODEHUCA) and its Panamanian counterparts CONADEHUPA and COPODEHUPA which sent teams of interviewers out into the "field of battle" last January 1990 to talk with the victims of this tragedy: those who saw, suffered and lost friends and family, homes and possessions. Because of the shock, pain and fear experienced by the victims, many were reluctant to give their names because of the ongoing presence of foreign troops. Yet their stories were forthcoming and are poignant and powerful in their simple honesty.

From her base in Costa Rica as head of CODEHUCA, Mirna Perla de Anaya—herself a victim of the war and repression in El Salvador (her husband as head of the non-governmental Human Rights Commission, Herbert Anaya, having been murdered in 1987)— refused to wait or be silent, sharing the information gathered and speaking out publically against the crimes of the December 20 invasion. The best way to honor these human rights organizations is to record one more of the numerous testimonies, as yet another example of Panamanian suffering and courage. The following testimony comes from a member of the oft-maligned Dignity Battalions ... from a soldier who later died in combat defending his beloved country:

December 24, 1989

Dear Sweetheart,

To describe what I have seen break's one's heart and makes me cry with pain and fury in light of all that has happened.

I believe I have started this letter badly, but the pain I feel is so great that I couldn't avoid it. Those of my people who are left, continue harassing the "gringos" and the possibility of their surrendering is very slight because their convictions are firm and they cannot accept the fact that "gringos" kill our people and that they go through the streets of our country as if they were loved.

The fighting is a case of "over-kill"—we are horribly overwhelmed by the power of their weaponry. When we would attack and then pull back, the USA would immediately come back with their helicopters and bombard the entire area with rockets and bullets, without caring about the civilian inhabitants. The gringos had no courage to attack the Battalions directly, but have used incredible amounts of new and high-tech weapons.

At night, they searched for us everywhere from their helicopters with infra-red spotlights. Wherever they thought we might be hiding, they would fire off a rocket with some chemical material.

Given that we have shot down some of their helicopters, they are now bombarding us with very fast A-37 fighter planes. These planes are far less accurate with their bombs but that isn't a problem for them, if the bomb falls on a house it doesn't seem to matter....

This has been a massacre. I don't have words to describe it. They killed two of my friends. They were with me and I couldn't get them out of there. I looked for an ambulance that was going by and when the ambulance went to get them, the USA troops opened fired on it.

They are savages. They have a sick fury (rabia enfermisa). They have massacred our people, our population like animals.

In their tanks, they have driven over bodies of Panamanians, without caring whether they were dead or wounded. They are just like or even worse than Hitler's Germans.

I am very disappointed about the Panamanian Defense Forces. They demonstrated that they had neither the preparation nor the disposition nor the conviction to defend our country from the gringo attack.

It's evident to me that the Dignity Battalions have all the necessary patriotic attributes to offer their lives in the name of liberty against the forces of injustice.... [12]

The *fraternity* expressed by international solidarity organizations reflects a second important ingredient in the process of Panama finding its new nationalist path. We often speak of solidarity in abstract terms, as if it were just an ideal or value, whereas in reality it usually represents very decisive and courageous acts of speaking out and taking risks in the face of potentially negative implications for one's life and relations. In the case of Mexican solidarity for the Panamanian people, forinstance, response came from over 300 groups: civic associations, human rights groups, popular organizations, trade unions, cultural associations and religious bodies. Following is a portion of their declaration, issued last January:

We denounce:

The invasion and occupation of Panamanian territory by the U.S. armed forces....

The transgressions of the Constitutional Charter of the Organization of the United Nations and the OAS which violate fundamental human rights and is an act against the self- determination of peoples;

The "smoke screen" created by the invasion of Panama which misdirects world attention away from the crimes committed against the Salvadoran people and the contra

aggression against Nicaragua, trying to cover them up....
We demand:

The immediate removal of North American invading troops from Panamanian territory and respect for the sovereignty and self-determination of all peoples....

Freeing of all prisoners detained by U.S. troops and payment for the damages caused in lives, housing and goods lost by the Panamanian population....

Free elections of those to govern the Panamanian people and the breaking of diplomatic relations with the Government imposed by the Bush administration....

We exhort:

All U.S. Congresspersons and all governments who defend the principle of respect for human rights to declare themselves in solidarity with our demands and requirements in the struggle for justice, freedom and peace for the Central American people....

All organizations of the civilian population throughout the world to denounce this trampling on the sovereign rights of Panama....

—Open Letter to U.S. Congress, the North American People, and All in Solidarity with the Defense of Human Rights, Justice, Freedom and Peace ... [13]

Finally, the *Love* expressed between North Americans and Panamanians in New York City during an evening of solidarity on Thursday, April 5, 1990, at New York Town Hall called "Voices of Panama," reflected the rising concern about what U.S. foreign policy is doing to the rights and dignity of the peoples of Latin America and the Caribbean. That event, sponsored the Independent Commission of Inquiry on the Invasion of Panama, which is headed by the Hon. Ramsey Clark, former U.S. Attorney General, proved this spirit is not dead. The 1,300 persons who attended with another 700 forced to remain outside on the street for lack of space, reflected the love and unity which thousands of U.S. citizens have for their Panamanian sisters and brothers in common opposition to the U.S. invasion.

Among the many speeches that evening, Olga Mejía, president of the National Human Rights Commission of Panama, gave one of the

most loving and determined talks of all. We end this report with some
of her words and a poem by Rafael Pena Arosemena.

Accept a most fraternal embrace on behalf of the Panamanian
children, youth, women, fathers and above all of the mothers
who know what life is and what it is to lose their most precious
loved ones. . . .

One hundred days after the invasion, the occupying army
continues to operate with impunity and the high cost in human
life still remains to be brought to light. . . .

The people who witnessed the charring and cremation of
bodies were prevented from attempting to identify the dead.
When the people of El Chorrillo tried to stop and identify the
bodies that lay in the streets, they were forced to move on. . . .

It is for this reason that the massacre of El Chorrillo and
against Panama must not be allowed to spread throughout
Central America and the Caribbean, nor to any other sister
country. . . .

Finally, with a strong embrace from all the "Voices of
Panama," we would like to express our gratitude for your
presence because it shows that your hearts and wills are with
us in the struggle against the unjust military invasion and
occupation of Panama.[14]

Epilogue
Rhythm & Challenge[15]

Rafael Pena Arosemena, Panamanian

RHYTHM ... SONG OF MY
LAND
PRESSURE ... DRUM
AGAINST THE WAR

My breast expanded
feels aflame
also my fists.

Today I Arise,
our dignity
is not a mourning
but love
for a sovereign country.

The aggression no longer
produces terror
of that genocidal empire
and in the morning

I arise
to look for a buck
for some food.

RHYTHM ... A SONG OF
    MY LAND
PRESSURE ... DRUM
    AGAINST THE WAR

I know that soon
I will see
my nation free
and sovereign.
I will not be a slave
of the empire.... I'm Panama-
    nian
from here to Chepigana.

RHYTHM ... A SONG OF
    MY LAND
PRESSURE ... DRUM
    AGAINST THE WAR

We will triumph over
this enormous spider's web
our hope
will be invincible.
We will dance in El Ancon,
dance when
the foreign barricade
has fallen.

A Free Nation
will be the fulfillment
of our
Torrijista struggle
and free too will be
the Canal
in a progressive land.

Against the empire
and its aggression
A RHYTHM PUSHING &
    CHALLENGING
is the voice
of a single heart
from here to there
and from the smallest shanty.

RHYTHM ... A SONG OF
    MY LAND
PRESSURE ... A DRUM
    AGAINST THE WAR

I'm a dancer
with dignity
who was born
in the heat
of a bloody sleep
inspired by the wind
which grew
from the pain
of a wounded nation.

THIS CHALLENGE OF THE
    RHYTHM
I offer to that genocidal gringo
that's how I'll dance
when they come to me
with yearning

and clarity
about where I'm headed.
My struggle to reclaim
is the love I give
to a sovereign nation.

RHYTHM ... SONG OF MY
   LAND
PUSHING ... A DRUM
   AGAINST THE WAR

Commentary & Call from *Dialogo Social*

Rafael Pena Arosemena reveals a style in his poetry for which we congratulate him. *Dialogo Social* calls on our Panamanian readers inside and country, to build up a new poetry, today more than ever. Let us express in verses our pain, experience and, more than anything, our hope for worthy and sovereign nation for generations. . . .

Notes

1. Association of National Security Alumni, *Unclassified*, Washington, D.C., April 1990, p. 6
2. Ibid., p. 7.
3. *First Principles*, Center for National Security Studies, Washington, D.C., Feb. 1990, p.1.
4. Ibid., p.7.1
5. Doug Vaugn, "Notes on the Invasion of Panama," The Christic Institute, Washington, D.C , Feb. 1990, pp. 3-4.
6. Catherine Sunshine, *The Caribbean: Survival, Struggle and Sovereignty*, EPICA, Washington, D.C., 2nd Ed., 1988, pp.124-130.
7. *Newsweek*, Feb. 15, 1990, "Drugs, Money and Death," p. 34.
8. Ibid., p.36.
9. *Opinion Publica*, CELA, August 1989, Panama,"Intervencion Armada en Panama," pp. 8-9.
10. Roger Fontaine, *Panama: After Noriega*, Council on Inter-American Security, Washington, D.C., 1990, pp. 48, 51-52.
11. *El Diario-La Prensa*, Panama, May 3, 1990, p. 11.
12. Jose de Jesus Martinez, *Ideario Omar Torrijos*, op. cit.,p. 109.
13. Ibid., p. 46.
14. CODEHUCA, *Testimonios*, Jan. 1990, op. cit., Doc. 3, pp. 1-4.
15. *Carta Abierta* by over 300 Mexican organizations, See: AFSC, Philadelphia, translation, Jan. 29, 1990, which document ends with the quote: "Democracy rises from the will and decision of its people not from the imposition of an imperialist army."
16. "Voices of Panama," Town Hall, New York, City, April 5, 1990, Presentation by Olga Mejia, President of the National Human Rights Commission of Panama, sponsored by the Independent Commission of Inquiry on the Invasion of Panama.
17. *Dialogo Social*, Panama, Feb/Mar 1990, "SALOMA Y DESAFIO," p. 8.

ADDENDA

1
Fifty U.S. Violations of Treaty with Panama

by Panamanian journalist Luis Restrepo

> *The country is a dream of a shared future; the country*
> *is, above all, hope of the future.*
> —Omar Torrijos

Introduction

A chapter in the important struggle for national integrity of Omar
Torrijos ended in September 7, 1977, when Omar Torrijos Herrera,
representing Panama, and the President of the United States of
America, James Carter, signed the Panama Canal Treaties at the
headquarters of the Organization of American States in Washington.

To the Panamanian people, it was a historic event, an undeniable
evidence of success for the new international policy of Panama
inaugurated by General Torrijos. That moment had a significant
importance ongoing struggle of Panamanians for their liberation, their
independence, and for strengthening their sovereignty.

We Panamanians were aware that without boasting, but with
resolution and dignity, the Republic of Panama and its leaders had
put aside the policy of diplomatic secrecy imposed by the United

States upon all negotiations carried out during this country with our country—a suitable policy to impose their interests—they wanted to maintain that secrecy at all costs during this historic moment.

The Panamanians realized then that Omar Torrijos had every reason to put aside the bilateral negotiations with the United States that were taking place at the "Panama Desk" in the State Department and look for international support for the Panamanian issue.

Torrijos started by strengthening domestic militancy. He fostered the participation of Students' Federation and the national labor movement, and incorporated the agricultural communities into the national struggle.

At that moment, with his domestic and international pilgrimage, Omar Torrijos was carrying out a long pilgrimage for a small country that spoke with the voice of a giant; he shouted the Panamanian truth that thus was made known in every part of the world; he converted the Panamanian creed in to the religion of many governments and hundreds of millions of people from all the nations of the planet.

Omar Torrijos dared to break the colonialist circle imposed on Panama by the United States. It is true as General Omar Torrijos stated, that not all the aspirations of the Panamanian people were being achieved—but steps were begun which would be taken further as the process of decolonization developed.

Experiences

The Panamanians considered that the Panama Canal and Canal Neutrality Torrijos-Carter Treaties were a positive step in the national liberation struggle as well as in the elimination of the colonialist enclave built by the United States in the core of our country.

We Panamanians understood that the United States, a powerful, imperialist and aggressive nation would not yield easily the benefits it had gained by its political, economic and military presence in the Republic of Panama. The Canal Zone in Panama fulfilled many purposes within the U.S. strategy of control over Latin American, especially Panama, Central America and the Caribbean, as well as for U.S. political, economic and military expansion in the Pacific Ocean.

The construction and subsequent administration of the Panama Canal allowed the United States to expand its world trade and spread its political, economic and military influence in areas as far away as Asia, Africa and the Middle East.

Despite the usually frustrating experiences of our country in the Canal relations with the U.S., we trusted once more in the honesty of the other party, and so believing, a pact between the two nations was negotiated and approved.

The truth was different. The ink used by U.S. President Jimmy Carter, who committed the honor of his nation by signing the canal treaties was still wet when the Congress of the United States, showing utter contempt for world opinion, passed the Panama Canal Law, better known as Law 96-70 on September 29, 1979.

The Southern Command

One of the most important commitments agreed upon between Panama and the United States in the Canal Treaties is the ending of the military presence of the U.S. in Panama by December 31, 1999.

Panama has been the site for one of the most important U.S. command posts in its world operations. The particular strategic objective of this command post is to control Central America and the Caribbean and to maintain direct contact with U.S. embassies and military organizations in South America.

According to General Wallace Nutting, former Commander in Chief of the Southern Command, "to move the Southern Command to another place of this continent will be highly expensive; furthermore, in no other place can it work with the efficiency required to control Latin American as it does in the Panamanian isthmus."

The United States never intended to hand over the Canal and that is the reason why it has always kept a militarization policy in the Panama Canal Administration. The key positions in the administration are held by armed forces men who "were removed from the army of the Navy" to accept those positions in the Canal Commission. The United States is exerting pressure on the Panamanian government so it will accept the renegotiation of the permanence of the Southern Command in Panama beyond the year 2000.

Despite all its pressures the United States has not accomplished that purpose. For that reason it has orchestrated a campaign of offensive and virulent allegations against General Manuel Antonio

Noriega, Command in Chief of the Defense Forces of Panama, who has taken on a nationalistic leadership which U.S. leaders find intolerable.

The assassination of General Torrijos and the violent campaign of defamation against General Noriego, the increasing violations of the canal treaties; the political, economic and diplomatic terrorism show that nothing will deter the United States in its determination to impose the limitless presence of the Southern Command in Panama.

Law 96-70

Law 96-70 was conceived, passed and applied with the worst intentions by the United States. It is a law that fosters and justifies up to aberrant extremes the overdoing of jurisdictional, operative and administrative powers by the government of the United States, which, through the approval and application of the above-mentioned law, violently disrupts the spirit and wording of the Torrijos-Carter Treaties.

It must be strongly stated that the promulgation and application of Law 96-70 has gravely and definitely affected most of the righteous claims of the Panamanian people in their generations-long struggle to take advantage of this important natural resource of our country.

Law 96-70 attempts to perpetuate the image of the Canal enclave. The United States has placed that law above the Panama Canal Treaties and has imposed schemes of the 1903 Treaty and other agreements and commitments that were abolished when the new Canal Treaties came into force.

Law 96-70 is an anti-juridical instrument which denies the Unites States' acknowledgement of the sovereignty of the Republic of Panama over its territory as specified in the preface of the Torrijos-Carter Treaties of the Panama Canal.

Regarding the Violations

The violations or infringements of the 1977 Panama Canal Treaty committed by the United States, can be grouped and then studies according to the objectives of such violations or infringements.

Some violations originate from the application of the United States

Congress Public Law 96-70 regarding the implementation of the Treaties. Other violations originate directly from U.S. government officials. Both can be grouped according to the aggression against the Republic of Panama as follows:

A) Organic Aspects, B) Labor Aspects, C) Financial Aspects, D) Jurisdictional Aspects.

The government of Panama has complained about these violations directly to the government of the United States. The same denunciations are being stated in all international forums: United Nations, Organization of American States, Non-Aligned Countries, etc.

The United States has not stopped his aggression against Panama. Violations of the Treaties are increasing as January 1, 1990 comes closer, the date on which, according to the agreement between the two nations, a Panamanian shall be appointed as Administrator of the Panama Canal.

1. Establishing a Panama Canal Commission in the U.S. executive branch, under the leadership and direct authority of the U.S. President, who will exercise his authority through the Secretary of Defense in spite of the fact that the Treaty very clearly establishes that this Agency will be under direction and authority of a Joint Board of Directors in which four Panamanians will participate.

2. To reduce the oversight function of the Board of Directors established by the Treaty to a mere supervisory role.

3. To subject the rulings of the Board of Directors to the approval of the Secretary of State.

4. To create the position of Chief Engineer not established by the Treaty, with functions to be prescribed by the President and which could be the same that are today carried out by the United States Administrator.

5. To diminish the authority of the Advisory Committee, converting it into a merely diplomatic forum.

6. To discriminate against the Panamanian representatives on the Board of Directors and on the Joint Commission for the Environment regarding travel expenses and fees.

7. To grant the U.S. Ambassador authority not agreed upon in the Treaty regarding the coordination of the transfer of duties to the Republic of Panama in accordance with the Treaties.

8. To subject the Panamanian employees of the Commission to the

labor laws of the United States, although the Treaties state that the terms and conditions of employment of such employees shall be approved by the Board of Directors of the Commission and will therefore be local.

9. To subject the employees of the Commission to a competitive system without giving consideration to the directives of the Treaty which calls for a growing participation of Panamanians in these jobs.

10. To leave open the possibility that the Administrator or Deputy Administrator of the Canal might be an active member of the United States Armed Forces.

11. To create a system of subsidies exclusively for the North Americans employed as functionaries, not contemplated in the Treaty.

12. To give preferential eligibility to United States war veterans, ignoring the principle of preferential eligibility for Panamanians as established in the Treaties.

13. To ignore festivals and national holidays established by Panamanian laws and instead to celebrate U.S. holidays and festivals.

14. To charge as operating costs for the Canal the amortization of the fund to pay advanced retirement due to those who worked for the Panama Canal Company and the Canal Zone Government, both of which no longer exist.

15. To charge as operating costs of the Commission allowances given to employees of the Panama Canal and which are not established in the stipulations of the Retirement Law of the Canal Zone.

16. To charge as operating costs for the Commission the purchase of artificial limbs and similar devices for those who were injured while working for the Panama Canal Company.

17. To create a Personal Policy Coordinating Board in which no Panamanians participate, which is not answerable to the Board of Directors and which is not contemplated in the Treaty.

18. To apply Title 5 of U.S. Code to the labor relations of the Commission, thus subjecting Panamanian employees to the authority of the U.S. Department of Labor and the National Labor Relations Board.

19. To place the administration of the finances of the Commission under the control of the U.S. Congress, which will not assign funds for use by the Commission, nor will allow the Commission to commit any funds unless those funds have been specifically authorized by U.S.

law.

20. To limit the financial responsibility of the United States in the Canal, by stating that no funds will be allocated for the use of the Commission during any fiscal year when there is a surplus income produced by the Canal.

21. To refuse to release from the united States Treasury the emergency funds of the Panama Canal in order to cope with emergencies such as the recent massive landslide in Cerro de Oro.

22. To create a system of accounting which goes beyond the Law of Accounting and Auditing of 1950 and which is not in accordance with generally accepted norms and practices of accounting.

23. To list capital investment as operating costs.

24. To charge as operating costs the depreciation of equipment and machinery of the old Panama Canal Company and which the Commission received through transfers or with titles of non-responsibility.

25. To exclude the Republic of Panama from the audit to determine the surplus to which Panama has a right by Treaties.

26. To charge as canal operating costs, public services such as education and health to Zone employees who are United States citizens.

27. To extend the use of the United States diplomatic pouches to include the personal correspondence of the Zone employees of the Canal and to bill this service as a Commission operating cost.

28. To charge as Commission operating costs the deficits of past fiscal years, thus affecting the surplus which ought to be paid to Panama as a result of operations of each fiscal year.

29. To prohibit the authorizations of tolls in tariffs calculated to cover the payments of surplus to Panama, which the Treaty does not prohibit.

30. To limit the responsibility of the commission for damages or losses caused by Canal workers to $50,000 and then to refuse to pay the Port Authority for damages in the ports beyond that amount.

31. To create in Panama a U.S. tribunal of investigation with the name of Local Inspectors Group which can summon witnesses, take depositions under oath, subpoena books and documents, pass judgements, and carry out other judicial proceedings.

32. To return to the United States all possessions and other

current assets of the Panama Canal Company on the day the treaty took effect and to give the Commission the right of use only. With this stipulation, the United States has been transferring to other U.S. agencies land and assets of the Canal with a free title, and will transfer all removable office equipment and machinery to other U.S. agencies at the expiration date of the Treaties.

33. To place under the authority of the President of the United States and not of the Board of Directors the right to establish and from time to time change the tolls tariffs and regulations for inspecting ships.

34. To prohibit tolls from being set at a level which would produce enough income to cover the payments of surplus agreed upon in the Treaty.

35. To charge to the operations of the Commission the interests "over the investment of the United States in the Panama Canal" and to unilaterally utilize a whimsical formula for charging interest.

36. To subject the change of the regulations of the Canal's waters to a judiciary meeting according to Chapter 7 Title 5 of the United States Code.

37. To grant the United States President authority to prescribe municipal and police regulations to be applied in Panama, such as the exclusion and dismissal of persons, the possession and use of alcoholic beverages, health and sanitation, use of aircraft, the guarding and penning of animals, the selling or use of fireworks, the protection of wildlife, hunting and fishing, the issuance of official and marine permits for ships crossing the Canal and adjacent waters, including the ports of Balboa and Cristobal.

38. To appoint an economist after qualified Panamanians had applied for that position.

39. To refuse to fly the Panamanian flag in the Commission's ships operating in Panamanian waters.

40. To maintain U.S. citizens in their jobs after their retirements when there were better qualified Panamanians.

41. To grant privileges for purchases in military PX's and the use of U.S. post offices to "Zonians" without any agreement with the Joint Committee.

42. To refuse to retain income tax from citizens of third countries who are working in the Canal.

43. To refuse to cooperate with Panamanian authorities, as established by the Treaty, in deducting payment for alimony and debts ordained by competent courts of justice in Panama from the salaries of Commission employees.

44. To establish mechanisms to eliminate positions vacated by United States citizens for the purpose of not employing qualified Panamanians. Such is the case of the Engineering and Construction Bureau.

45. To maintain preferential fees for United States citizens for housing, electricity, water, education and health care not authorized by the Treaty.

46. To charge as Canal operating expense the salaries of domestic employees serving the Commission Administrator, expenses not established in the Treaties.

47. To maintain illegal mechanisms for substituting during the temporary absence of top employees, even if there are qualified Panamanians, by always choosing United States citizens even if they lack the necessary qualifications.

48. To refuse to employ Panamanians in the office of the Commission in the United States.

49. To administrating the Commission from Washington, bypassing the authority of the Administration.

50. To create a special police corps carrying guns and wearing uniforms as an act of provocation to the Panamanian police who are in charge of keeping the peace by constitution and by Treaty mandate. This is an act for provoking violence.

2
The Real Drug Dealers in Panama

Carlos Wesley, Senior Analyst for Central American and the Caribbean

As you know, on December 20, 1989, in what could accurately be said to be the first test of President George Bush's new World Order, the armed forces of the United States—some 30,000 strong, armed with the most sophisticated weapons in the world, from stealth fighter bombers to laser rays, and even chemical weapons—achieved a great military victory against the Panamanian Defense Forces led by Gen. Manuel Noriega, an army exactly the size of the Chicago police department, and probably not as well armed.

What were the reasons for that invasion? There were no death squads in Panama. Despite all the propaganda against noriega, it was never claimed that the invading forces had liberated a *single* political prisoner held by Panama's Defense Forces. One has to admit, that the Panamanian Defense Forces under noriega had a better human rights record than the Los Angeles Police Department under Daryl Gates.

So, what was the invasion about?

In his speech on December 20, 1989, after the troops had gone into action, President Bush said: "The goals of the United States have been to safeguard the lives of Americans, to defend democracy in Panama, to combat drug trafficking and to protect the integrity of the Panama Canal Treaty."

Let us look at those assertions one by one. Let us examine what has happened in Panama since the invasion, in light of the goals Bush claimed he wanted to achieve.

From the outset let me say that we will be looking at this through the eyes of a Panamanian, my eyes, not from the sort of academic standpoint you might be more accustomed to.

First assertion: The invasion was to combat drug trafficking.

Well, the big headline in Latin America yesterday Friday and today, Saturday, April 6, was that another report from the DEA said that the U.S.-installed president Guillermo Endara was an officer of at least 6 companies involved in laundering drug money. The money, according to the reports, was from a drug ring run by Colombians Augusto Falcon and Salvador Magluta, which allegedly smuggled *one ton* of cocaine each and every month into Florida, during at least a decade, up to 1987. Endara said he left the companies, on whose board he sat with other members of his law firm, in 1987. But the reports say he remained on the board until at least December of last year, 1990. Other members of Endara law include Menalco Solis— who runs the CIA-trained National Security and Defense Council and the Institutional Protection Service—and Hernan Delgado, Endara's key presidential advisor, who was the chairman of the companies charged with money laundering.

It is not the first time Endara has been found to be linked to drug-money laundering. He was a co-owner and on the board of Banco Interoceanico, which was ordered liquidated last month. According to U.S. authorities, Interoceanico was laundering funds for the drug mafias, and had even set up special branches in 1989 just to handle the huge inflow of drug funds, specially that coming from its main customer, Medellin cocaine cartel kingpin, Gonzalo Rodrigez Gacha, now dead.

Among the banks named yesterday, there are the Banco General, Banco de Colombia, Union Bank of Switzerland, Banco Aleman, Primer Banco de Ahorros, Sudameris, Banaico and Banco del Istmo. Most of them are run by the people the U.S. deployed against Noriega and later installed as the government of Panama. For example, Banco del Istmo belongs to Gabriel Lewis Galindo, who is being touted as a potential replacement for the Endara-led troika, if and when the Bush administration decides it's time for a change in Panama.

U.S. authorities had information about these individuals alleged illegal activities, long before they were recruited to the anti-Noriega operation, and most assuredly, long before it decided to install them as the government of Panama.

Besides Endara, other officials of the U.S.-installed Panamanian government known to be tied to drug trafficking and/or to drug money laundering include:

Second Vice president Guillermo "Billy" Ford was a co-owner, with politicians Carlos Rodriguez, who was Endara's ambassador to Washington, and Bobby Eisenmann, publisher of *La Prensa*, of Dadeland National Bank of Miami. Dadeland Bank was the institution charged by prosecutors with laundering the funds for drug trafficker Antonio "Tony" Fernandez, sentenced in 1985 to 50 years in jail in the famous Dadeland Bank of Florida-Steven Samos money-laundering case.

Dadeland Bank was also the laundromat of choice of Medellin Cartel Money launderer Gonzalo Mora, Jr., who pled guilty in 1989 to drug money laundering charges in Florida.

Also, according to the *Miami Herald* of January 5, 1990, convicted

Medellin Cartel Money launderer, Ramon Milian Rodriguez said he laundered millions of dollars in the 1980s through a company owned by Ford's brother, henry, and that Billy, the now Vicepresident, also helped his money-laundering operations.

The article said the Vice President's nephew, Haime Ford Lara, was a schoolmate of Milian Rodriguez. It was Jaime Ford Lara who introduced Milian Rodriguez to the Ford family. Ford Lara was named by the Endara government to run the Colon Free Zone.

Attorney General Rogelio Cruz, who is supposed to be the country's top law enforcement official, was an officer of First Interamericas Bank, co-owned by Gilberto Rodriguez Orejuela of the Cali Cartel and Jorge Ochoa, of the Medellin Cartel. Also on the board of First Interamericas, which was shut down by Noriega in a joint operation with the DEA in 1984, was jaime Arias Calderon, brother of Guillermo Arias Calderon, First Vice President in the U.S.-installed government of Panama. Jaime Arias Calderon is admittedly, the chief financial conduit of brother Ricardo's political operations.

The jointly owned money-laundering institution of the Medellin and Cali cocaine cartel, First Interamericas, has provided other alumnae to the roster of the current Panamanian government, including Treasury Minister Mario Galindo and the Chief Justice of the Supreme Court, Carlos Lucas Lopez Tejada.

Given that this is the make up of the government installed in Panama since the invasion, it should come as no surprise then, that as London's *The Independent* reported on March 5: "Statistics now indicate that since General Noriega's departure, cocaine trafficking has, in fact, prospered" in Panama. A few days earlier, on March 1, the U.S. Department of State admitted in a report that drug-money laundering is also up, at least to the levels of 1989, when George Bush ordered the invasion of the country, killing at least 4,000 if not many more Panamanians.

But, you don't need the DEA or the State Department or even Carlos Wesley to tell you if getting rid of noriega advanced the war on drugs. There is a very simple test. Has the flow of drugs gone down in Washington D.C. or in your city or on your campus? Has the number of drug-related murders and other crimes decreased since the U.S. forces went after Noriega and confiscated 50 kilos of cornmeal tamales in December 1989?

I am sure the answer is no.

Second assertion: to defend democracy in Panama.
Let me be blunt about it. The U.S. has established a military dictatorship in Panama. Panamanian waters are now patrolled by the U.S. Coast Guard. Panama City, Colon and other cities are subject to so-called anti-crime sweeps by U.S. troops.

Earlier this year, there were congressional and local elections in Panama. To get out the vote in favor of the U.S.-installed government (which lost, by the way), candidates supported by the Americans got to campaign in U.S. military helicopters, according to one of the few issues of the opposition newspaper *El Periodico* that managed to reach the public. Since it is not possible to teach the natives good old U.S. of A. electioneering without a little porkbarreling, U.S. occupation authorities in Panama sent out the bulldozers to the town of Nombre de Dios, in the province of Colon, where U.S. Army engineers launched operation "Fuerte Caminos 91." Dubbed as "the largest civic action program" undertaken by SouthCom in all of Ibero-America, the operation was inaugurated with the kind of fanfare that would have caused the envy of a Chicago ward heeler from the old days.

The 142nd, a U.S. Army medical battalion, dispensed vaccines and pushed pills to peasants in the most remote villages. The 470th intelligence brigade interrogated voters daily.

As war was about to break in the Persian Gulf, U.S. troops again deployed in force in the provinces of Chiriqui, Bocas del Toro, Panama and Colon, because of Panama's large Arab population. And, as most of you know, just this past December 5, U.S. troops deployed in full combat gear into Panama City, supposedly to put down an alleged coup by the former chief of police, Eduardo Herrera.

Every government office in Panama has U.S. military officers assigned to it, from Endara's presidency on down. These are officers from the Pentagon's so-called Civic Action-Country Area Team, or CA-CAT. They are CA-CAT officers assigned to each ministry, all the way down to municipalities and even to police precincts in Panama City. This degree of military control is unheard of in Panama's history. Even under the military governments of Gen. Noriega and his predecessors, all the way back to the leader of the 1968 revolution, Gen. Omar Torrijos, the day-to-day running of the government and most policy decision making was in the hands of Panamanian civilians.

The American officers are training the police forces, and reeducating the former members of the Panamanian Defense Forces—PDF—that were kept on the new Fuerza Publica. As they have explained their mission, the idea is to tell the Panamanian people, via television, that they should forget the issue of the invasion, and concentrate their energies on rebuilding the national identity.

This was described in somewhat blunter terms by American General Marc Cisneros, the former head of U.S. Army South. The PDF, he said "needed an enema." Insofar as the general Panamanian population, the American general Cisneros was also very explicit: "They need to have a little change in mind set," he said. Panamanian, he added, "need to have a little infusion of Anglo values."

Race

What are some of those values? Well, take racism.

Before the invasion, the Noriega government was a model of affirmative action, only no one in Panama made any fuss about it.

The president was Francisco Rodriguez, a mestizo; the Chief of the Supreme Court was Marisol Reyes de Vazques, a woman. The head of the electoral Tribunal, a position of equal rank as the chief justice of the Supreme Court, was also a woman.

The minister of Government and Justice, who is considered the top official of the cabinet, was Renato Pereira, a black man; the Foreign Minister was Leonardo Kam, of Chinese decent; the Treasury Minister was Orville Goodin, a black man; the Minister of Labor was George Fisher, another black man, and so on down the line. As the PDF, Noriega was very visibly a mestizo and the rest of the high command included several black men, including the head of the air force, such as it was, and a couple of Chinese.

Who were they replaced by? There is only one woman and one black in the Cabinet, and it happens to be the same person: Education Minister Ada de Gordon. Every other top official in the U.S.-installed government of Panama just so happens to be a white male, and most are related to each other. I already mentioned that Ford's nephew, Jaime Ford Lara is head of the Colon Free Zone. Endara's uncle is head of the Social Security Administration, and so on and so forth.

What the U.S. invasion installed as the government of Panama was the oligarchic comprador class which traditionally ruled Panama until the 1968 Torrijista revolution. These oligarchs, known in Panama as "rabiblancos," or white tails, are incapable of governing because, since the establishment of the Republic in 1903 with the assistance of Teddy Roosevelt, the Americans always governed for them.

Their pathetic showing during the more than 30 months that preceded the invasion, during which time the U.S. Embassy tried to use them to lead an opposition against Noriega, proved their unwillingness to fight for anything. Virtually every strike against Noriega planned by the strategists at the U.S. embassy fizzled when this gang refused to shut down their businesses for fear of losing a day's profits. Such is their contempt for the blacks and mestizos who make up the majority of Panama's population, that they were never able to organize a mass base. So seldom were they willing to abandon the air-conditioned comfort of their cars to hold a demonstration that the international press took to referring to them as "BMW revolutionaries."

Freedom of the Press

There is no free press. Under the so-called dictatorship of Noriega, Panamanians had more access to the media. Since the U.S. was so keen on getting Noriega, anyone who had a complaint against the General, no matter how unfounded, was virtually guaranteed prime-time coverage by ABC, CBC, NBC, CNN and NPR. Nowadays, no one gives a hoot.

Take the case of broadcaster Balbino "Nino" Macias, the owner of Radio Millonaria. He decided to test the government's commitment to democracy by opening his microphone to the public in February of last year. Things were ok until he decided to hold an informal poll. When it turned out the 8 of every 10 callers was against the invasion and the U.S. installed government, there were moves to shut down the station. Macias responded by chaining himself to the studio, and the government backed down—for a while. All of a sudden, Macias found himself facing enormous electric and telephone bills from the government-owned utilities. He had no choice. He toned down his anti-government broadcasts.

Journalist Escolastico Calvo, the former publisher of *Critica*, *Matutino* and *La Republica*, was detained by U.S. troops at the time of the invasion and sent to a concentration camp. On what authority, it is not known. He was later transferred to Panamanian authorities who kept him in jail, without trial, until a few months ago, when he was finally let go "for humanitarian reasons" after an international campaign for his release. Why was he not tried? Well, the only charges the government thought it could make stick were for misdemeanors. "I have insisted they try me to get this over with. Even if they manage to convict me, the most I could be sentenced to is to pay a fine of a few hundred dollars," Calvo told me last week.

The same with former legislator and university professor Rigoberto Paredes, who has been held without trial since the invasion, first at the American concentration camp and then by the government.

El Periodico came out as a clandestine weekly from time to time. But when it tried to make it as a daily earlier this year, the motors of its press burned down by sudden power surges. It is now shut while its publishers try to raise money to buy the needed replacement parts.

What Panamanians now have is what passes for a free press in the United States. That sort of freedom of the press is useful, as A. J. Liebling once said, only if you own one. Since in Panama the only ones who can afford to publish a newspaper are the rabiblancos, only they can say what they want, but only so long as it is within the established parameters. True dissent does not exist.

No Rule of Law

How can it, when the rule of law is ignored? Members of the legislature are supposed to be immune from arrest when the National Legislative Assembly is in session. Only if the legislative body agrees to lifting a member's parliamentary immunity can that member be arrested and subjected to prosecution, regardless of the charge. Yet, opposition legislator Elias Castillo was jailed at the start of the current legislative session, and the government did not even seek to get his immunity lifted, which would have been a mere formality since they command a majority in the parliament.

Following a 100,000-person-strong "right to life" march this past December 4, which was organized by the labor movement to protest the growing unemployment the plans by the government to sell of the state sector at bargain basement prices, every single one of the labor leaders involved was fired, down to the level of shop-stewards, and arrest orders were issued for 100 of the top leaders. It turns out that the labor leaders had the law on their side. The march took place after working hours, and they were engaged in an activity protected by the labor code, and by the other laws, up to and including the Constitution of Panama.

Not to worry. The U.S.-installed government ordered them fired anyway, and then got the Legislative Assembly to approve a law, ex post facto, giving them the legal authority to carry out the dismissals.

Destroying Torrijos

I want to say something about the on-going campaign to turn the late nationalist leader Omar Torrijos into a non person. His name has been removed from Panama City's international airport, from schools, museums and other public buildings. School teachers have been instructed to refer to Torrijos as a "dictator."

Most Panamanian revere Torrijos because of his contributions to the nation's development. During his government, from 1968 to 1972, electrification was extended to most of the country. Highways, hospitals, schools, water works, telephone networks, and whole towns were built. Illiteracy was nearly eradicated. Persons from the poorest lawyers were given the opportunity for higher education. And, most important, he ended Panama's semi-colonial status by successfully negotiating the 1977 Panama Canal treaties.

According to labor leader Mauro Murillo, Panamanians "lived moments of splendor, of advancement, or progress during the Torrijos era." Murillo, who heads Panama's National Workers Federation (CNTP) and who is also a vice president of the Latin American Communications Workers, has said that under Torrijos and his successor, Noriega, "workers, peasants and the people in general participated in running the state, because we were consulted and our opinions were taken into account."

The offensive against Panamanian nationalism, he says, is to lay the groundwork to refinance the foreign debt, and to impose the structural adjustments of the International Monetary Fund and the World

Bank. That would entail privatization of all state companies, reducing the minimum wage, and doing away with the right of collective bargaining, he said.

Destroy the Economy

The destruction caused by the invasion and the preceding 2 years of economic warfare cost Panama up to $7 billion, according to officials of the former government, and at least $3 billion, according to officials of the Endara government. After promising $2 and then $1 billion dollars, the U.S. government finally approved just $460 million. Of that, only $42 million was slated for so-called humanitarian aid, and a few million more for other government operations. The greater portion of the funds are staying right here in the United States to pay some of the $800 million in arrears on Panama's foreign debt, which is now close to $6 billion dollars. Even the money earmarked to go to Panama has been held back by the Bush administration to force the Endara government to sign the Mutual Legal Assistance Pact.

But that's not all. The U.S. admitted having stolen $400 million of Panama's own money under the economic sanctions against Noriega. Part of that money was used to finance shady operations by the fictitious government nominally run by former president Eric Delvalle out of his condo in Coconut Grove, Florida. But, after the invasion, instead of returning what was left to the Endara regime, the U.S. government held on to the greater portion and sent it off to the banks, again to help clear up Panama's arrears.

Fifteen months after the invasion, there are still some 2,000 persons of the estimated 40,000 left homeless by the U.S. bombing of El Chorrillo are living in cubicles in the abandoned hangars of the former U.S. Air Force base at Albrook. Most of the other persons displaced from El Chorrillo were forced to make their own arrangements to find shelter. U.S. AID allocated $6,500 per family for replacement housing, but that does not even compensate for the personal property they lost, much less buys replacement housing. In fact, it is far below what those people are entitled to as indemnization under the rules of war. El Chorrillo is slated to undergo what is known in the U.S. as gentrification.

The government rescinded a law adopted by the previous military governments that froze land prices in Chorrillo at $40-80 per square meter. Without the freeze, said Raul Figueroa the Housing Minister, land prices in El Chorrillo will eventually zoom up to $900 per square meter, placing it out of the reach of the former residents, whose monthly income averages an estimated $160 per month.

In a recent report, U.S. AID said that because of "criticism that attempts were being made to prevent residents to return to what some considered a prime downtown area," it was forced to offer the choice of building low income housing in El Chorrillo. But, says AID, those who choose to go back to Chorrillo will have to wait another 1 or 2 more years before an apartment is available, and then the apartments will sell for $12,000, almost twice as much as the $6,500 housing grant.

More than one third of Panama's total labor force is unemployed. For the first time in decades, there is now a problem of infant malnourishment, according to Endara's own Health Minister. The same official has also warned that Panama is going to be hit by the cholera epidemic now sweeping across South America.

Yet, the entirety of the government's economic program is oriented towards selling off state enterprises at bargain basement prices, and paying the debt, no matter what it takes. That policy was made in the U.S. As an official of the Bush administration told the *Los Angeles Times* soon after the invasion, "economic recovery should be the country's number 2 goal. Panama's first priority, says the U.S. is to pay off its foreign debt." The American official, according to the newspaper, said that if Panama spent money creating jobs, "You will have created in the long run a basket case. If you spend the money on public works, it will take away from debt payment."

When Vice President Arias Calderon suggested last week that maybe the government should pay some attention to the social debt before it lost all support, Comptroller Ruben Dario Carles replied that's nonsense: Peru's Alan Garcia tried that and look where it got him. We have an obligation to pay the debt and that's it, said Carlos.

This, of course, is all in the name of the "free market" economy promoted by Bush. But even super-capitalists such as Dulcidio Gonzalez, the staunchly pro-American former head of Panama's National Council of Private Enterprise (CONEP), has said the National Strategy for Economic Development and Modernization imposed on the government of Panama by the Bush administration means "the death of private enterprise."

According to Gonzalez, "this damned economic plan seems to have been drafted by Martians after an all-night marijuana-smoking party."

The third assertion: to protect the integrity of the treaties.

The 1977 Panama Canal treaties call for the United States to turn over the Panama Canal to the Republic of Panama on December 31, 1999. At the same time, the U.S. is supposed to shut down its military bases in that country.

A little over 2 weeks ago, on March 21, Sen. Larry Craig (R-Id.) introduced a concurrent resolution calling on George Bush to renegotiate the Panama Canal Treaties to maintain a U.S. military presence there, "because the Republic of Panama has dissolved its defense forces and has no standing army or other defense forces capable of defending the Panama Canal from aggressors and therefore remains vulnerable to attach both from inside and outside of Panama." First the U.S. armtwists Panama into disarming itself, then a resolution is submitted to Congress that "calls on President George Bush to renegotiate the Panama Canal Treaties to permit the United States Armed Forces to remain in Panama beyond Dec. 31, 1999 and to permit the U.S. to act independently to continue to protect the Panama Canal."

The concurrent resolution, introduced in the House by Rep. Philip Crane (R-Ill.), is backed by Senate Minority Leader Bob Dole, which means the Bush White House is also behind it.

By one of those coincidences of history, on the same day, on March 21, the U.S.-installed government sent a number of proposed amendments to Panama's Constitution to the National Legislature. The most important of those amendments would forever abolish Panama's right to an army.

Conclusion

It is clear that none of the three main reasons Bush gave for the invasion has succeeded. Far from combating drugs, the invasion installed a more corrupt government in power in Panama with predictable results: more drugs and more drug money laundering. The invasion, in fact, put in a drug government that has made Panama safe for drugs. Instead of democracy, Panama is now governed by a U.S. military dictatorship that does not allow a free press, ignores the rule of law and has no respect for human rights. Insofar as the third assertion, to protect the integrity of the Panama Canal Treaties, the Bush administration has de facto torn-up the treaties through the invasion and subsequent occupation, and it's now proceeding to nullify those treatise de jure.

So every one of the aims to the invasion has been botched. One must conclude that either the Bush administration is the most incompetent bunch of buffoons ever to occupy the White House or—and this is my own personal conviction—from the beginning, the Bush administration has approached Panama as a laboratory to perform the experiments in how to set up the New World Order, the results of which we have now seen applied to Iraq, and will likely soon see extended to other nations of the Third World.

This report is a paper presented by Carlos Wesley of the Executive Intelligence Review *at the Latin American Studies Association (LASA) conference held in Washington, D.C., in April 1991.*

BIBLIOGRAPHY

Americas Watch, *Human Rights in Panama*, New York, April, 1988.

Arias Madrid, Harmodio, *El Canal de Panama*, Editora Panama-America, Panama, 1957.

Arosemena, Jorge, "La United Fruit Co. Enclave Colonial Panameno," *Tareas*, No. 27, Panama, December 1973.

Bolanos, Felix E., "Las Luchas Reinvindicatorias Panamenas," *Relaciones Entre Panama y los Estados Unidos*, Biblioteca Nueno Panama, Panama, 1974.

Bunau-Varilla, Phillippe, *Panama: The Creation, Destruction and Resurrection*, McBride, Nast & Co., New York, 1920.

Bunker, Ellsworth, "Panama and the United States: Toward a New Relationship," U.S. Department of State, Bureau of Public Affairs, Washington, D.C., May 1975.

Burns, E. Bradford, "Panama's Struggle for Independence," *Current History*, Jan. 1974.

Castillero Calvo, Alfredo, "Transitismo y Dependencia: El Caso del Itsmo de Panama," *Relaciones Entre Panama y Los Estado Unidos*, Biblioteca Nuevo de Panama, Panama, 1974.

Castillero Pimentel, Ernesto, *Panama y los Estados Unidos*, Litho-Impresora de Panama, Panama, 1953.

CEASPA, "El Canal de Panama y los Intereses Japoneses en America Latina" by Charlotte Elton, No. 6, September 1987, Panama.

CEASPA, *Este Pais: Mes a Mes*, Panama, February, 1990.

CELA, *Tareas*, Guillermo Castro, "Politica y cultura: Santa Fe II" and Marco Gandasegui, "Santa Fe II: Una introduccion a la democracia imperial," No. 72, Panama, May-August 1989.

CELA, *Tareas*, Juan Jovane, "La agresion a la via interoceanica," No. 73, Panama, 1989.

Cox, Robert G., "Choices for Partnership or Bloodshed in Panama," *The Americas in a Changing World,* Center for Inter-American Relations, New York, 1975.

Dialogo Social, "El Pueblo Esta Descontento," and "Se Esta Forjando Una Nacion," February-March 1990, Nos. 229-230, Panama.

Dingus, John, *Our Man in Panama,* Random House, New York, 1990.

Ealy, Lawrence O., *Yangui Politics and the Isthmian Canal,* University of Pennsylvania, University Park, PA., 1971.

EPICA, *Panama: Sovereignty for a Land Divided,* Washington D.C., 1976.

Fontaine, Roger, *Panama: After Noriega,* Council for Inter-American Security, Washington, D.C., 1990.

Gandasegui, Marco A., "La Lucha de Clases y la Zona del Canal," *Tareas,* Panama, January-April, 1975.

Gandasegui, Marco A., *Panama: Crisis Politica y Agresion Economica en Panama,* CELA, Second Edition, 1989, Panama.

Green, Graham, *Getting to Know the General,* New York, 1984.

Gomez and Ortega, *Desarrollo, Crisis, Deuda y Polirtica Economica en Panama,* Panama, 1985.

Gomes and Salazar, *Panama 1988,* "Que Hacer Con La Deuda Externa?" and "El Sistemna Monetario y la Crisis de Circulante en Panama," Panama, 1988.

Gonzalez, Simeon, "La Crisis del Torrijismo y Las Elecciones de 1984," Ediciones Horizonte, Panama, 1985.

Gorostiaga, Xabier, "La Zona del Canal y el Subdesarrollo Panameno: Diez Tesis Sobre el Enclave Canalero," *Tareas,* Panama, 1975.

Gorostiaga, Xabier, "Evaluacion de la Potencialidad Economica de la Zona del Canal de Panama y los Estados Unidos," Ediciones Aude, Aude, Universidad de Panama, Panama, 1973.

Guagnini, Luis, "Panama: La Guardia Nacional," *Dominical-El Panama, America,* Panama, 1975.

Hogan, J. Michael, *The Panama Canal in American Politics,* Carbondale, Ill., 1986.

House of Representatives, U.S. Congress, "A New Panama Canal Treaty: A Latin American imperative," U.S. Government Printing Office, Washington, D.C., 1976.

Illueca, Jorge, *Las Negociaciones sobre el Canal de Panama,* Universidad Nacional, Panama, 1973.

La Feber, Walter, *The Panama Canal: The Crisis in Historical Perspective,* Updated Version, 1989, Oxford University Press, New York.

Leis, Raul, *Comando Sur: Poder Hostil,* CEASPA, 1985, Second Edition, 1985.

Liss, Sheldon B., *The Canal,* University of Notre Dame Press, Notre Dame, Indiana, 1967.

Liss, Sheldon B., "Panama, the United States and the Canal: Ten Years Later," *Panama: Sovereignty for a Land Divided,* op. cit.

Marquez, Gabriel Garcia, "Cuatro Preguntas al General Torrijos," Ediciones Reforma Educativa, No. 4, Ministry of Education, Government of Panama, Panama, 1975.

Marques, Jaime, *Panama en la Encrucijada: Colonia o Nacion?* Editorial Panama, 1989.

Martinez, Jose de Jesus, *Ideario Omar Torrijos,* Editorial Universitaria Centroamericana (EDUCA), San Jose, Costa Rica, 1982.

Martinez, Jose de Jusus, *Mi General Torrijos,* Editorial Nueva Nicaragua, Managua, Nicaragua, 1987.

Martinez Ortega, Aristides, "Panama Explodes: The 1964 Flag Riots," reproduced in English in *Panama: Sovereignty for a Land Divided,* from "Naracion de los Sucesos de Enero de 1964," *Loteria,* No. 191, Panama, October 1971.

McDonald, Vincent P., "The Panama Canal for Panamanians," *Military Review,* Professional Journal of the U.S. Army, Vol. LV, No. 12, Washington, D.C., December 1975.

McGrath, Bishop Marcos, "The Canal Question: A Christian View," Carnegie Endowment for International Peace, Washington, D.C., September 1974.

NACLA, *Panama,* Vol. 8, No. 7, East Coast Division, New York, September 1974.

Neruda, Pablo, "History of a Canal," *El Canal de Panama,* Madrid, 1972.

Opazo Bernales, Andres, *Panama: La Iglesia y la Luche de los Pobres,* DEI, San Jose, Costa Rica, 1988.

Opinion Publica, CELA, Panama, February 1990.

Panama y la Frutera: Una Batalla Contra El Colonialismo, Editorial Universitario de Panama, Panama, 1974.

Pensamiento Propio, CRIES, Managua, Noicartagua, No. 67, Jan/Feb 1990.

Pedrishi, Carlos Bolivar, "El Nacionalismo Panameno y la Cuestion Canalera," *Tareas,* Panama, 1975.

Priestly, George, *Military Government and Popular Participation in Panama: The Torrijos Regime,* Boulder, Colo., 1986.

Ricord, Humberto, "El Tratado Remoin-Eisenhower," *Relaciones Entre Panama y los Estados Unidos,* op. cit.

Roosevelt, Theodore, *State Papers as Governor and President,* H. Hegadorn Co., New York, 1920.

Selser, Gregorio, *El Rapto de Panama,* EDUCA, San Jose, 1982.

Selser, Gregorio, *Panama: Erase Un Pais A Un Canal Pegado,* Universidad Obrera de Mexico, San Ildefonso, Mexico, 1989.

Shirmer, Boone, "Panama and the U.S.," *Resist,* Cambridge, Mass., February 1976.

Soler, Ricuarte, "La Independencia de Panama y Colombia," *Relaciones Entre Panama y los Estados Unidos,* op. cit.

Sunshine, Catherine, *The Caribbean: Survival, Struggle and Sovereignty,* EPICA, op. cit., Updated Version 1988, "Panama."

Tack, Juan Antonio, "Informative Letter from the Minister of Foreign Affairs to the U.N. Secretary General U Thant," Government of Panama, Ministerio de Relaciones Exteriores, Panama, 1971.

Torrijos Herrera, Omar, *La Batalla de Panama,* Eudeba, Buenos Aires, Argentina, 1973.

Torrijos Herrera, Omar, *Nuestra Revolucion,* Ministerio de Relaciones Exteriores, Government of Panama, Panama, 1974.

Turner, D. H., *Tratado Fatal!* Editorial Progresiva, Mexico, 1964.

Vance, Cyrus R., *Hard Choices,* New York, 1983.

Weeks and Zimbalist, "The Failure of Intervention in Panama," *Third World Quarterly,* XI, January 1989.

Yau, Julio, *El Canal de Panama: Calvario de un Pueblo,* Editorial Mediteraneo, Madrid, 1972.